Y0-EEF-686

Derrick R. Fries, Ph.D.

Educating At-Risk and Special Education Boys
A Great American K-12 Tragedy

Custom Edition for Eastern Michigan University

Cover Art: *Contemplative Figures*, by Robin McDonald-Foley

Pearson Learning Solutions, 501 Boylston Street, Suite 900, Boston, MA 02116
A Pearson Education Company
www.pearsoned.com

Printed in the United States of America

38 2023

000200010271795272

RM/KE

ISBN 10: 1-269-44487-5
ISBN 13: 978-1-269-44487-3

Educating At-Risk and Special Education Boys: A Great American K-12 Tragedy

By: Derrick R. Fries, Ph.D.

Educating At-Risk and Special Education Boys: A Great American K-12 Tragedy

Table of Contents

Acknowledgements

In the course of writing this book I am surprised as I look back at the nearly 40 years that I have worked in education gathering empirical information on male students in the K-12 Educational System. I began my career as a regular education teacher at Pontiac Northern High School in Pontiac, Michigan. During my time at Pontiac, I gathered important information about urban issues and boys. Throughout several more years of public school teaching experiences, and a year-long stint in the unemployment line, I finished my Masters in Special Education, specializing in Emotionally Impaired students. From 1979-1992, I worked at Seaholm High School in the Birmingham Public School System, located in Birmingham, Michigan. At Seaholm, I was a Special Education teacher, department head, and a NASA state finalist for the teacher in space program. The leadership at Seaholm, including Mr. James Wallendorf and Mr. John Schuster, both administrative personnel, and my experiences with the issues facing the male students made a lasting impression on me. After finishing my doctoral degree at the University of Michigan in 1993 I became Assistant Principal at Covington Middle School and worked under the guidance of an outstanding Principal, Bill Blackwell.

After my days in Birmingham Public Schools, I began a principalship at Avondale Middle School where I worked with a wonderful Superintendent named Dr. Jim Bird. I was also fortunate enough to have a wonderful, collaborative and insightful relationship with Mr. John Pagel. Much of this book reflects on the troubled crusade that boys experienced in Middle School during my 7 years as Middle School Principal. After my principalship I became Deputy Superintendent for Avondale Schools which included duties as Curriculum Director and Special Education Director. In my Avondale days, two of the most outstanding teachers included P.E. teacher Mr. Ray Went and Science Teacher, Mr. Greg Bien.

My days of competing in sailboat races, triathlons and marathons have continued, uninterrupted, since my collegiate athletic days. These sports-related experiences have created immensely strong bonds with other males in my life, including Mr. Tom LaBelle and my two younger brothers Mark and Kurt Fries. Additionally, my own three sons Drew, Liam and Aidan have inspired me to write this book. In watching their unique development and religious experiences in sports, they have opened new doorways to male bonds. I am extremely thankful to my parents Glenn and Mary Jo Fries for the many sports opportunities they provided me in my childhood. In closing, none of the above could have occurred without the undaunted support of my one-in-a-billion wife, Katherine. To her I am forever indebted.

Introduction

American schools invest a considerable amount of time, effort and resources into the development of a productive human being. It is difficult to believe that after 13 years of education, time, and resources invested in at-risk and special education boys, that we have such a poor rate of return. For instance, the average student in a public school system, over the course of a 13 year education costs approximately $100,000. All educators hope to see this investment in each student pay off in the form of further education and/or successful employment. However, only about 70% of all boys graduate from high school and much of each $100,000 investment goes to waste. Boys, who drop out of high school at age 16, cost the tax payer approximately $250,000-$300,000 in additional expenses that are functions of negative outcomes. These negative outcomes manifest themselves in several forms, varied levels of incarceration (cost of jail and prison time), or social welfare programs to assist students who cannot or will not seek gainful employment. By grade three, most educators can predict, with nearly 95% accuracy, those boys most likely to drop out of high school. Consequently, without a high school diploma, these boys will be sentenced to a life of poverty and will be a life-long burden on the state. To date, this drop out crisis has not been examined as a singular gender issue caused by our inability to successfully educate at-risk and special education boys. Much of the dropout issue has to do with self-esteem and ego management issues for young males who do not find success or belonging in our highly social secondary schools. We all need to take a share of the responsibility to change this poor paradigm that causes hardships for millions of boys each year. This book addresses many of the reasons why this great American tragedy exists and offers productive and meaningful solutions.

Chapter 1 – No Girls in Sight

It was shortly after lunch period on a cold January day. I was the principal of Avondale Middle School, a suburban school north of Detroit, Michigan. As I returned to my office I found six boys waiting for a talk with the principal. Two of the six had been involved in a scuffle; the other four were there for other various reasons. However, like most days, there were no girls in sight. The bell for fifth period had just rung and I had the laborious chore of dealing with six boys, each with a different version of what happened during lunch period. Five of the six had been to my office at least one time prior and three of the six I had seen more than seven times each since the beginning of the school year. I chose to see the one student who I had not seen before first with the hope of hearing his story and getting him back to class quickly. Sometimes all it takes is one contact with a boy, and some meaningful consequences from the principal, to sort out his problems. This one encounter could turn the tide and possibly keep this boy out of trouble, and out of the office, in the future. The other five boys were gravitating towards chronic behavioral problems in school. Although one could obviously question my logic, missing class time for them was necessary and they would have to wait.

Zack...

As I brought him into the office and sat him down across from my desk, his body language read passive and non-confrontational. His behavior indicated that he was beginning to ask himself, "What in the heck am I doing in the principal's office?" I allowed him to tell his side of the story while I glanced at the referral slip issued by the cafeteria worker. The referral slip simply said "seventh time in line without lunch money." "We have given Zack seven peanut butter and jelly sandwiches and free milk, something has to be done." As I read the referral I said to myself, "Now this is unchartered water; seven times not paying for lunch." Usually the referrals from the cafeteria come down after the fourth or fifth time. All the possible scenarios quickly ran through my mind as to what might be happening: A) He is buying and trading things on the bus ride to school, giving up his lunch money. B) Someone is bullying him for his lunch money. C) He really is not getting any lunch money from home. D) He is simply saving it for some other purchase or function. I finally asked Zack, "Why have you gone to the lunch line for seven consecutive days, taken complimentary food from the lunch ladies, and not paid for it?" Zack's response was simple, "Dr. Fries, I am sorry I am just not getting any money from home and I can't borrow any more money from my friends." I said, "Zack are you telling me that your parents are sending you to school knowing you are not eating a lunch?" "Well kind of," he replied. "I haven't earned my lunch money because I haven't kept up with my chores at home." Now, in the back of my mind, I attempted to resolve this problem while trying to be relatively expedient because there were five more boys waiting outside my office. However, Zack's issues were deeper than I initially thought. "Zack, what is your home phone number?" I asked. He said, "We don't have a home phone anymore, my mom just has a cell phone". "All right, can I have her number please?" Zack gave me his mom's cell phone number. I called his mom but I was sent to her voicemail. I left a voice message and sent Zack out of the office with his referral slip and instructions to get it signed by his mom. I also requested an explanation from her as to how we were going to work through the issue, get Zack lunch each day, and help him focus on his academics. "Zack, as soon as you get off of the bus in the morning, what are you going to do?" I asked. "Bring you the signed referral slip with an explanation from my mom," was his response. "Good job Zack," I replied, "I will see you in the morning." Off he went to his fifth hour class, approximately seven minutes late, over an issue that apparently stemmed from home.

Danny and Tyrell...

The next two boys had referral slips from a worker who cleaned the cafeteria. The slips stated, "Both boys refused to pick up trash from table after lunch, chronic problem, and have been warned numerous times to pick up their trash." For the sake of expedience I chose to see both boys at the same time. They both sat at the same table, which is always a bit of a risk, since, as a team, they will often collaborate their stories and beef up their bravado. Bringing two boys in together generally meant a lower likelihood of accepting responsibility and a higher probability of projecting masculinity and dominance. I said that I was embarrassed that they were missing school time over this extremely silly issue, read the referral form to the boys, and asked them why they were sent to my office. In my head I was ready for the typical answer of, "It wasn't our stuff that was left on the table and floor". Danny's response surprised me when he said "It is not my job to pick up the trash, the cafeteria ladies get paid for it" Danny's, "I am the king and everyone around me should act as my servant," response is not unusual for boys in middle school. I replied to Danny, "What did you have for lunch today?" And his response was, "A Sunny D orange drink and a bag of chips." "So Danny," I replied, "Your garbage is less than one handful of stuff that would take less than three seconds to walk to the trash can to dispose of?" I had seen Danny before and it was clear that he was starving for approval and affection. He would often back himself into a corner knowing that, for him, negative attention was better than no attention at all. Of course, he was expecting my typical response. I would normally give him a lunch detail picking up garbage during the next day's lunch. Danny would thrive on such punishments as he would be seen as the "bad kid" to his peers which would garner more attention and satisfy his craving to be noticed. This is an inherent trait found in a lot of boys. Like Danny, many boys find themselves struggling to carve out a niche for their fragile egos. "Danny," I said, "Tomorrow you are going to report to the office. I am going to go get you your lunch and you are going to pick up trash on the outside of the building in a designated area." Danny responded, "Oh no, dude." I quickly corrected him, "Danny, you know my name and you are going to address me as Dr. Fries, sir." "If you have an issue with that then you can join me the next day too." Now this was an important interchange between me and Danny. My response was from a dominant male prospective that essentially said there is one alpha male running this school and it is Dr. Fries. But the message is really more than that. Although it will be interpreted by Danny as "Dr. Fries isn't going to take any guff and he is an authority that will win this match." At its core, it is a message of civility, respect and appropriately addressing people with proper names and dignified language. The key to effective discipline of boys hinges on when to provide strong authority and when to provide degrees of empathy, sensitivity and emotional support. At the age of twelve most boys understand how to respond only from one vantage point. The ability to turn different degrees of emotional responses on or off is not taught to boys. On the other hand, this is a technique that girls easily learn since they are allowed to demonstrate various degrees of emotional response. Conversely, boys are often taught that they can only show one degree of emotional response; illustrated by Danny's quip, "Oh no, dude." I sent Danny back to class and looked forward to seeing him the next day at lunch time.

Danny's peer, Tyrell, had a much different explanation when I asked why he would not pick up his trash. Tyrell looked down at the floor and would not make eye contact. He simply said, "I don't know." Tyrell's response was an attempt to shut the conversation down and avoid any degree of responsibility. My response to Tyrell was, "Tyrell look at me when you speak." "If you want to resolve this matter quickly you know the correct things to say and how to change your behavior." "What do you have to say?" I asked. Asking Tyrell to make eye contact and connect with me emotionally was a bit of a risk. I crossed the line of emotional consecutiveness and he could have easily withdrawn further. He could also, so I hoped, step up and say, "I'm sorry Dr. Fries and it won't happen again." I was fortunate that Tyrell's was a positive, "I will pick up the trash." "Tyrell, is there an apology in there?" I asked. "And how much longer are you going to pick up the trash?" He continued in a soft monotone voice, "I'm sorry; I'll pick it up the rest of the school year." Notice that Tyrell didn't try to connect with me emotionally. He simply wanted to get the problem over and go back to class. It was too risky for his boyhood ego to make any attempts to connect emotionally with me, the principal. For Tyrell, it was easier to divert the problem, give an expected response and move on. I sent Tyrell back to class with a pass.

Willy and Chris…

My next two boys, Willy and Chris, got into a scuffle while playing basketball outside on a twenty-four-degree January day. There was a group of about eight boys that were outside, with school permission, playing basketball in the cold January air. Apparently Chris had inadvertently stepped on Willy's foot. Then, in a subsequent play, there was a long debate over a three point shot. As a result, there were some ill feelings between the boys, a pushing match ensued, but no punches were thrown. I gave each boy a chance to describe his side of the story, in my office, sitting next to each other. Both boys started with a similar response, "Oh it was nothing." Willy and Chris both knew that if they admitted to a physical, pushing and shoving altercation it would probably get both of them a day or two of suspension from school. The response, that "it was nothing," was their way of avoiding the real issue. For young boys, on the basketball court, it comes down to one universal truth, "I'm a bigger 'badass' basketball player than you." Both Willy and Chris were, otherwise, relatively good kids who hid tempers and anger issues that they had difficulty resolving. Although both boys wanted to plead, "Please don't call my parents," neither had the nerve to do so. Of course, contacting parents after a fight was one thing that I always did. However, I decided to withhold suspension and parental contact from both Willy and Chris because they appeared to show remorse. As an alternative, I assigned them five straight school days to sit at a lunch table alone, just the two of them. I instructed them to work through their differences and made it clear that the conflict between the two of them would either be resolved in my office or at the lunch table. Whichever method they chose, they had to produce a written statement for me at the end of the fifth day. My message was simple, "you **are** going to work things out." I placed the two boys on stage during lunch time knowing that most of the school knew why they were sitting together. These two boys, with deep anger issues, would probably spend about three seconds saying, "Ok, we are not going to let it happen again," and that is all they would talk about during their five days of lunch time isolation. My forced-resolution exercise was, of course, only a temporary fix. One look at Willy's face and I knew in his heart that all he wanted to say was, "Dr. Fries, this is gay" – he had used that expression in the past on another resolution piece. However, this time he abstained from his usual tactics and agreed that he would work on the written resolution.

Thomas…

After spending forty minutes with five out of the six boys, fifth period was coming to a close and I was about to see my final student, Thomas. Thomas was a special needs, emotionally impaired student who was sent to my office for drawing a violent and graphic picture during lunch. He was brought to the office by a teacher who was walking through the cafeteria and noticed his drawing. On the drawing Thomas wrote, "Death to C. C." The picture, drawn with pencil, depicted gory, detailed graphics of seven bloody knives sticking into the body of a middle-aged man. When I recovered the drawing from my secretary, I asked Thomas about it. He calmly stated, "I was just having some fun with the drawing". This was Thomas's eighth contact with my office since early September. Thomas's background was riddled with problems. Specifically, when he was in the sixth grade he brought a two and a half inch knife to school. I asked Thomas to stay in my office for a brief moment, left the door open and quickly went down to his locker to investigate whether he had any knives or weapons in his possession. Upon my return, I reminded Thomas of our previous discussions about drawing inappropriate violence and gore in school. I told him that if he wanted to do this at home, with permission from his parents, that was fine. His response was simple and casual, "I was bored and I was trying to stay out of trouble, Dr. Fries." The fifth period bell was about to ring as I ended my discussion with Thomas. I then spoke to his special education teacher and his mother.

Fifth period flew by with six issues and six boys all from the social, lunch period. Later, as sixth period ended, I walked into the hallway outside my office again; there were no girls in sight. Reflecting on the 6 boys that I saw, 2 were special ed., 3 were at-risk students with low grade point averages, and 1 was a regular ed. boy who made a habit of showing up in the office. This day was like most days as a Middle School Principal, full of unwavering boy issues.

Chapter 2 – What Schools Don't Teach Boys

Brandon...

It was a warm September day when I walked into a third-grade classroom taught by Mrs. Thomas. I sat down to observe a sixty minute writing lesson with her third grade students in preparation for the upcoming state assessment test. Watching Mrs. Thomas interact with all of her students, I could feel the stress in her voice and see the tension in her eyes. The students' performance on this annual assessment, mandated by No Child Left Behind (NCLB), weighed heavily on her mind. Mrs. Thomas, a veteran teacher, had been working on assessment preparation with students for nearly a decade. The lesson for the day was construction of sentences developing a topic theme, and writing clearly, including grammar, punctuation and spelling. Within a couple of minutes, my focus was drawn to Brandon. He wrote left-handed and was moving slower than many of his female peers. He was seated among his fellow classmates in typical elementary school "pod" fashion. Pods usually consist of three or four desks facing each other. In this particular pod there were three girls and Brandon. Directly across from Brandon sat Tiffany. The contrast between the two students' writing skills was striking, even alarming. Tiffany grabbed her pencil with a relaxed style and fluently put pencil to paper. She could write well, spell correctly and seemed to possess all the necessary fine motor skills for writing. Brandon struggled to grip his pencil properly and clearly lacked the fine motor controls that Tiffany possessed. It was obvious that Brandon was not worried about spelling and sentence structure. He simply held his pencil and, almost absentmindedly, scribbled his thoughts on the page in an attempt to construct letters, words and passable sentences. In Mrs. Thomas's classroom there were twenty-seven students, fourteen boys and thirteen girls. The upcoming state-standardized test was four weeks away and Brandon was clearly struggling with the simple task of putting words together on paper. His fine motor skills had clearly not developed yet and he was left to fend for himself. Conversely, Tiffany was developing sentences and unique thoughts while writing freely with proper fine motor skills. I was able to deduce his issues with a simple classroom observation yet Brandon was still expected to get the same passing scores on the state assessment test as Tiffany. The differences in development between students like Brandon and Tiffany are not unique. Yet we continue lowering standards to equalize grades across varying levels of intellectual physical development. This creates a bigger gap between boys and girls and inappropriately emphasizes differences in the ways that boys and girls mature, grow up and develop their intellectual facilities.

The differences in how we look at boys and girls, in our current educational system, reflect the major symbolic differentials in performance between boys and girls. Throughout the school years these differences manifest themselves in the form of boys starting behind girls in many different developmental categories. By forcing boys to do things they are not, developmentally speaking, ready for, we perpetuate five major educational problems as students work their way through elementary, middle, high, and post-secondary school experiences. These five problem areas are as follows: emotional and behavioral disorders drop out and graduation difficulties, self-esteem and personal confidence issues, adolescent decision making problems, and shortfalls in post-secondary education and employment. Many boys are just not ready to take State Assessments in writing in the third grade, which creates more stress in the life of teachers like Mrs. Thomas.

Richard...

Richard was a regular education student with educated parents that were involved with school functions. Richard had difficulty in Mrs. Thomas's class, especially in the afternoon following lunch. He was often listed on Mrs. Thomas's Progress Reports and Report Card Comments as being somewhat disruptive and off-task. Generally, Richard would eat his lunch, clean up after himself and then run out to the short, ten minute, outdoor recess following lunch. Richard loved all types of games and activities. Often times, at lunch, he would play a pickup game of soccer and in the fall he would play some touch football. During recess, with only a limited time to engage in these activities, Richard would start his physical "zone play" while becoming emotionally and mentally engulfed in his games. As the bell rang to return to Mrs. Thomas's class to start the afternoon writing assignments, Richard was always the last one off the playground. Mrs. Thomas ate her lunch in the staff work room and did not have lunch time duty. Rather, the supervision of the playground rested on a noon-time aid. Since Mrs. Thomas was not out on the playground, she missed Richard's engulfing, playful, "zone behavior," which was the highlight of his day. After lunch, as writing assignments began, Richard's mind was still engaged in the soccer or football game activity. He simply had difficulty making the transition back to academia because of his love for outside activity. However, the school interpreted this as off-task and sometimes disruptive behavior. After 30 minutes of redirecting, Richard would eventually settle into his writing assignment. In the 30 minutes needed to make the successful transition, Richard's enjoyment of his 3rd grade class deteriorated because he was not afforded sufficient recreation time to blow off steam and pent-up energy. This deficiency left a negative impression on Richard and his relationship with Mrs. Thomas suffered. If Mrs. Thomas only knew that he was having troubles with his transitions, not with his attitude towards writing, circumstances may have been different. When the warmer months started in April and May, Richard's transitional problems elevated. Mrs. Thomas suggested that Richard and his parents should consider medication, but what Richard needed was 45 minutes of exercise each day to blow off the steam that comes from being a third grader forced to sit still for 6 hours a day.

Elementary School Environments that Create Emotional-Behavioral Disorders

Johnny...

His name was Johnny; he was a second grader that had many emotional and behavioral disorders that would often manifest during structured, school settings. Johnny's disorders included defiant behavior against authority, inability to sit still and follow directions, and generally disruptive behavior. He also had a tendency to overreact to normal emotional situations. Needless to say, Johnny was a real handful for his third grade teacher. When he was two years old Johnny's parents divorced and his mom moved three times before he entered **the third grade.** Due to the distance between his mom and dad, he had very little contact with his biological father; his mother remarried. Johnny did not participate in any after school activities. The previous summer Johnny was not provided with any specific, focused, organized activities other than attempting to have fun around his neighborhood. Johnny's second grade teacher, Ms. Mart, also experienced a number of behavioral problems resulting in many classroom disruptions. It is difficult enough for a second grade teacher to keep her class focused on the daily lesson but nearly impossible when she is forced to juggle the needs of a special ed. student. After a number of interventions, Ms. Mart referred Johnny to the teacher's assistance team. This was a team of experts in the school that helped the teachers who struggled with difficult and challenging students. It was Ms. Mart's professional opinion that Johnny's reading, math and writing performance was far below grade level expectations. After a couple different attempts at individual tutoring and extra help, the assistance team decided to request a special education referral, and consent for testing from Johnny's parents. Since first grade Johnny had 27 office contacts and 4 days of out of school suspension for mostly physical altercations. The special education referral and testing would look at the possibility of diagnosing Johnny as an "emotionally impaired," (E.I.) student (In some states E.I. is referred to as emotional behavior disorder (EBD)). The E.I. designation would provide Johnny with extra classroom assistance. In order to conduct E.I. testing, the school must meet with the parents to get approval and a referral signature. During Johnny's E.I. meeting, which occurred in the middle of his third grade year, Johnny's mother refused to agree to the test. She didn't believe that Johnny needed any extra help or assistance, or that he had emotional problems that interfered with school. The good faith effort, on behalf of the school district, to get Johnny a full scale evaluation and some extra help in the classroom, was denied by Johnny's own mother. During this important meeting with Johnny's mother, the biological and step-dad were also invited. Neither one attended this meeting. A year later, Johnny found himself older, stronger and more physically aggressive, but still struggling with the same disruptive behaviors in the classroom. Johnny's fourth grade teacher, Mrs. Look, also attempted an E.I. recommendation, hoping to convince Johnny's mother that testing would be in Johnny's best interest. Throughout the United States, approximately 5% of the students that are categorized special education are also categorized as E.I., or EBD. Of the 5% diagnosed as E.I., approximately 80% are boys. Johnny's situation is typical of many boys around the United

States. Often in the early developmental stages an important male role model is missing from a boy's life. In Johnny's situation, in her best attempts, his mother was unable to fill that gap and as a result he acted out with aggressive and disruptive behaviors that affected him for the rest of his academic life. Without counseling, strong interventions or social work assistance, it was likely that Johnny would fall farther behind and cause greater disruptions in school. The incidents requiring discipline would continue, directly proportional to his disruptions, and would likely result in suspensions and other school-wide problems that would steer him toward the "drop out" category. Johnny is a prime example of a third grade boy crying out for help and yet he was not able to receive the help he needed.

Student Confidence and Self Esteem

For years I have had the privilege, in my educational experience, to glance over the grade books of early elementary teachers. I always enjoyed looking at grades and seeing the great differences between girls and boys, both on their assignment papers and the over all grades. Although grades themselves are only one important piece in developing student confidence and self-esteem, they are a very important indicator that sets future progress and trends. Recently I walked through an elementary school and looked at twenty-seven papers on the wall outside of a second grade classroom; the students wrote about their favorite summer time activities. Each of the twenty-seven papers was posted above the lockers in the hallway and neatly arranged on colored paper. The first name of each student was clearly identified on the top upper right of the paper. As I glanced through, looking at the papers, I could see such huge differences in writing skills. Most girls' papers were written with beautiful penmanship, thoughts were clearly developed, and fine motor skills were evident. Occasionally a boy's name would appear on a well written paper, but more often than not, somewhere near each girl's paper was a boy's that was written so poorly that it was difficult to make out letters, words, punctuation and any form of sentence structure. Self-esteem issues start early for boys. As they struggle to keep up with the pressures of subjects such as writing, thinking skills, reading and math, often times they lag behind. Once this lag occurs, unlike their female counterparts, it affects many boys' self-esteem and self-confidence. Once self-esteem and confidence has eroded away, established as a baseline level by the teacher, it will take years of time and effort for the boys to recover and figure out where they actually fall on the grade performance scale. Generally speaking, kids are smart enough to figure out and sort out their academic abilities. Within the first couple weeks of school, students know who is the smartest in the class and who gets the worst grades in each classroom. Often, as a result, boys with lower confidence and self-esteem fall to the wrong side of the fence and resort to getting attention through negative means. One of the worst mistakes we make with boys in elementary schools is not telling them that their fine motor skills develop slower than girls. Boys need to know that it is OK if they are falling slightly behind. The baseline for boys should be established against other similarly situated boys, not against girls. If we continue to use gender mixed classes then negative male self-esteem and self-confidence patterns, a function of falling behind girls, will continue to devastate class after class of boys. Some boys will have the ability to outgrow their self-esteem issues through other avenues like art, music, sports or outdoor activities. However, as much as we want it to be true, not all parents value leisure, recreation and sports that might allow boys to excel. Students who are deprived of extracurricular activities receive a double blow to their self-esteem. If they are slow in writing skills and other academic areas then they have no other opportunities to perform well and stand out. As a result, frustrations develop and students often act out in inappropriate ways that often manifest via behavioral difficulties. Consequently, behavioral difficulties are systemically connected to the fact that boys are not biologically ready to perform some of the skills that our school systems mandate.

One of the most confusing and difficult parts of school is the way that elementary classrooms are organized. Over the last couple of decades we have organized classrooms into desk arrangements referred to as "pods." Pods are best described as a group of four, five or six desks put together so students can sit near one another in small groups. This is an important new piece of the socialization for elementary students because it is different than the way schools delivered instruction for the previous sixty years. The development of pods emphasizes cooperation and group work which are important lifelong functions. However, the assessment, grading, progress and the performance of students is still measured on individual terms. Very seldom can you find any measurements in elementary schools that evaluate the performance of the collective pod and the five or six people working together as a team. Certainly this can occur on individual projects where the pod may work together to solve a problem but there are no formalized assessments that measure the collective work of a pod. The pod concept does translate to the professional world where teams often work on engineering and important solutions together and are often measured by team performance and function. However, the pod concept does have unintended consequences for boys who are suffering from self-esteem issues and academic problems. Working together sends a mixed message to boys in an already confusing elementary school structure. Boys are told that they must work in teams but they are evaluated on an individual basis. If we are going to send the right message to students then every report card in every elementary school in America should contain a grading scale that represents the ability to work in a group or in some sort of group dynamic process. This will allow students with lower than average self-esteem to get an "A+" in working collaboratively, in a group, and contributing as an equal partner to the group's overall outcome. It can be structured as a strength-based, positive support model, where different individuals bring different skills to the group's final project. This would be a big relief for many of our boys.

Boys and Decision Making

Throughout the school day, boys and girls are faced with many different types of decisions. This is a natural process in growing up and learning how to cope with day-to-day living opportunities.

As a natural part of American society, students are faced with many excellent choices, ex: what to buy for lunch, which after school activities to participate in, who to be friends with or what to do on the weekends. School structure focuses on what I refer to as "F-cubed," or facts, figures and fudge. For me this is one of the values of K through 12, education. Many of the facts and figures that students learn from class instruction will fall by the wayside in a matter of months. There is also the fudge factor which includes taking up time to get through a class period and/or school day. One of the important differences we know about boys and girls is the development of their decision making skills and emotional intelligence; emotional intelligence is part of their over-all maturity. How boys relate to their peers depends on their social skills, ability to solve conflicts, ability to stabilize, and other important respect characteristics that also translate into employment and function in the real world. However, schools spend little, if any time, focusing on these important human and dynamic characteristics. If one thinks about his employment experiences, the people that are successful in the adult, professional, employment world are those who are able to master their emotional intelligence. These people have good interaction skills, can communicate clearly, have a level head, and all the important ingredients necessary to be successful in the employment world. We also know that people generally get fired, not because of working confidence, but because of problems with emotions, intelligence, peer interaction, motivation, and other more human types of characteristics. This is a very important piece for the employment world, as more and more parts of our culture are working in teams and focusing on peer interactions. However, this aspect of evaluation and grading is totally void in the elementary, middle and high school sectors. Additionally, we know that girls develop their emotional intelligence, peer interactions and social maturity, much faster than boys. One of the very last parts of the brain to develop for males is their emotional intelligence. Some males are still developing all through their adult lives while others may develop appropriate and satisfactory emotional intelligence as early as sixteen or seventeen. However, most males struggle to develop the appropriate maturation skills, a deficiency that hinders their ability to be successful, professionally, well into their mid-twenties. This is one of the important factors in explaining why boys act impulsively, are more often labeled ADHD, and have more negative conflicts in school than girls. Girls can easily master the emotional intelligence piece much better than boys. Females are better equipped to understand our mass media culture that promotes social and emotional development while boys, without adequate development of emotional intelligence, will struggle with many mixed messages from our mass media culture. Some of these messages encourage boys to be masculine, strong in sports, and show little emotion. While other messages tell boys to be sturdy like an oak; the stoic boy that is strong, stable and mature. Still other messages preach that boys should show their epithetic, sensitive side. It is certainly preferable and an important piece of boyhood to learn empathy skills. However, there is little instruction in school to encourage boys to develop empathy for other boys, girls and worldly issues. An important part of anyone's mental health and success is the ability to develop empathy skills. This will make a person better in the world of employment and help them tolerate differences between all types of people.

In the last few decades, there has been a noticeable change in the way boys go through school. It has become evident that boys have established a real niche in school that being *bad* is good. This new model correlates with our mass-media culture. From TV and movies to videogames, many students who have not established a foundation through parental guidance and/or a social niche, turn to mass-media as a way of life. This brings us to the importance of the relationship between school officials and boys. As I discussed earlier, boys will often develop adverse relationships with school personnel to maintain their "badness" and receive negative attention. It seems that the new normal is to oppose authority, seek negative attention, and cause general irritations throughout the school day. This default niche of negative behavior too often appeals to a significant percentage of boys. In most high schools and middle schools, approximately 15% of boys fall into this negative arena.

Let's take the example of Henry. Throughout elementary and middle school, when I first met Henry, as his principal, he struggled. His dad was nowhere to be found while mom only had a high school diploma and had little control over Henry as he grew up through the elementary grades. In my opinion, Henry and his mom both had a substance abuse problem that started with mom smoking cigarettes and allowing Henry to do the same. This served as a gateway to smoking and, later on, selling marijuana. It came as no surprise that Henry performed poorly in school. His lacking performance was not a matter of substandard intellect, but more of general motivation. He struggled with reading skills and written expression, as boys often do, but he also found himself getting further and further behind in all areas. As a result of this, he became disenfranchised with school. Later, when I asked him why he ultimately dropped out of high school, he replied that he was "bored." It is typical for boys to deny the real reason they gravitate towards the side of "being bad is good." The foundation for why Henry ended up making many poor decisions was based on two factors: low reading skills that were never remediated, and lack of parental support. Many days, Henry would come into school, glassy eyed and stoned at 7:40 in the morning. One day, using my detective skills, I brought Henry down to the office and asked him to take off his shoes. Although he was generally compliant, it was clear, this particular day, that opposition was his course of action. However, after he finally removed his shoes, I found two marijuana cigarettes in a slit in his high-top. Before I checked the second shoe I asked Henry if I would find any more marijuana cigarettes. Of course, his answer was no. Sure enough there was two more marijuana cigarettes in the inside slit of his other tennis shoe. Having to deal with a long-term suspension was not an issue for Henry; as a matter of fact, it was a reward. He could stay home, get high, and work on distribution. But this, of course, would put him further behind in school and it was apparent, as his drug problem worsened, that he was not going to finish high school. At age 15½ he ended up dropping out of high school, citing the excuse, "nobody likes me and I'm bored;" Henry continued his ways of selling illegal drugs. Recently, I had the chance to interview Henry in the Upper Peninsula of Michigan where he is currently serving a long-term prison sentence. Upon his interview, now at age 26, he reflected on a couple of important factors. First, that he indeed had a reading problem and that was the real reason why he struggled in school and second, he had little or no parental guidance.

"If only I could have figured school out," he stated. "And you, Dr. Fries, I know you really tried to help me." "You tried to get me help and you encouraged me." "I know how much you disliked suspending me when you caught me with marijuana." "I haven't had many people who have really tried to help me." "I want to thank you for that." "Hopefully after I get out of prison, I will do better." "I want to be an auto mechanic." Currently, Henry is working on his GED in prison, but still needs to work on overcoming some of his reading difficulties before he will be successful.

Being bad is a constant mistake both for boys and our American society in general. Schools attempt to help, but with old fashioned delivery models, the male prison populations are rising. Ask any middle school, elementary, or high school principal and they will quickly identify the top 20 kids in their school that have taken on the "being bad is good" syndrome.

Chapter 3: Dropouts and More Dropouts

The next time you get a chance to sit through a high school graduation ceremony look at the nicely printed program in your hands and count the number of girls compared to boys. Across all 50 states, only 75% of the students who start high school will actually walk across the stage and graduate 4 years later. Of the 25% that drop out in the US, the vast majority are boys.

Michigan Graduation Rates

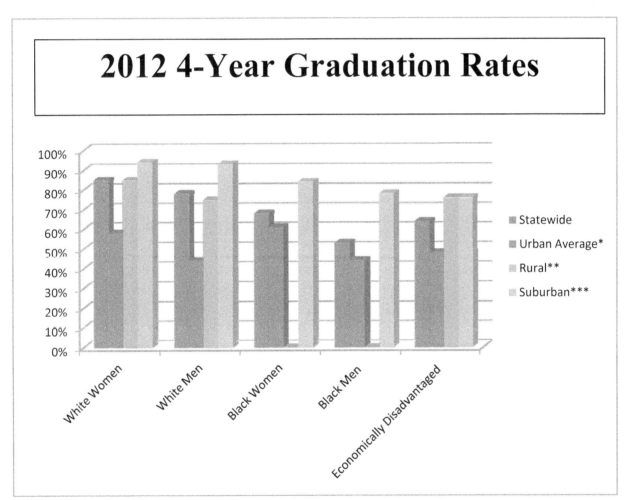

(**Source:** Michigan Center for Educational Performance & Information, 2012, State of Michigan 2012 Cohort Four-Year, 2011 Cohort Five-Year and 2010 Six-Year Graduation and Dropout Rate including Subgroups, 2013)

For many boys, by the time they enter high school and deal with the increased difficulty in curriculum and accountability standards, it just becomes overwhelming. They drop out, and most of them never return. A clear unintended consequence of the federal law, "No Child Left Behind" passed under President G.W. Bush, dropout rates have steadily increased as middle school and high school teachers continue to push increased academic rigor in the hopes of improving test scores. Though this is certainly appropriate for many parts of the student population, particularly girls, at risk boys create an even bigger divide. To complicate matters even worse, many of the students who do drop out have other emotional, or social, behavioral issues that go along with their "being bad" syndrome. Therefore, when they do drop out, not only does a poor test score walk out of the door, but generally behavior problems leave too. It is often an incentive for administrative staff to push these students out the door to get rid of their bad test scores and numerous headaches. Since difficult male students are disassociated with school, uninterested and uninvolved, few school personnel are willing to advocate for them. Conversely, gifted students, special ed students, and students who excel at extracurricular activities all have advocates within the system. Disassociated boys clearly feel these messages and quickly dissolve themselves of any responsibility to, or relationship with, their local school. Based on their attitude towards school, lack of parent involvement and poor performance in core academic areas, most trained professionals in education can spot these students as early as the first and second grades. By fourth grade, it is clear, in any test performance profile, which boys are most likely to fall by the wayside.

Since the 1950's the dropout rate in the US has improved. Looking ahead to the year 2020, at the current rate of improvement, we could get the US Graduation Rate above 80%. This would be a big improvement over the current rate; however, one dropout is too many. The HS diploma is just the starting block in getting noble employment in today's culture. In 1950 a HS diploma was a real accomplishment but today's associate degree from a community college is the new equal for getting a job.

State of Michigan 2012 Cohort 4-Year Graduation and Dropout Rate

Final Results

| District / Building Name (Code) | Totals | | | | Cohort Status | | | | Graduation Rate | Dropout Rate |
	First Time 9th Grade in Fall 2008	(+)Transfers In	(-)Transfers Out & Exempt	Cohort	On-Track Graduated	Dropouts (Reported & MER)	Off-Track Cont.	Other Completer (GED, etc.)		
State	127,284	7,844	5,439	129,689	98,881	13,884	15,203	1,721	76.24%	10.71%

(**Source:** Michigan Center for Educational Performance & Information, 2012, State of Michigan 2012 Cohort Four-Year, 2011 Cohort Five-Year and 2010 Six-Year Graduation and Dropout Rate including Subgroups, 2013)

* The Urban Average is based on a sampling of 7 school districts in varying regions across the State of Michigan. Those Districts are; Battle Creek, Flint, Grand Rapids, Jackson, Lansing, Muskegon and Saginaw.
** The Rural Average is based on a sampling of 7 school districts in varying regions across the State of Michigan. Those Districts are; Clare Public, West-Branch-Rose City, Hastings Area Schools, Stockbridge, Dowagiac, Wayland Union and Charlotte Public.
*** The Suburban Average is based on a sampling of 7 school districts in varying regions across the State of Michigan. Those Districts are; Grosse Pointe, Troy, East Lansing, East Grand Rapids, Birmingham, Ann Arbor, Bloomfield Hills.

Failure of Interventions

By the time fourth grade comes around, it is clear which students are going to be able to meet instructional standards. Most talented principals, teachers, and special education staff can easily profile and identify which students are likely to have serious problems in obtaining a high school diploma. However, the vast majority of school systems, in excess of 97%, fail to identify any interventions for these students. Whether the school district is focused on sorting and selecting students based on achievement pieces or states simply have educational budget concerns, these students are often left to fend for themselves. Approximately 70% of these disenfranchised students are boys. As long as the push for accountability standards and emphasis on learning facts and figures continues to be a high priority in this nation, these problems will persist. The average graduation rate for boys and girls in the United States is approximately 70%. This means that roughly one in four students who enter high school will not graduate with their class. Yet there are little or no interventions available to rescue failing boys. Some high schools are graduating less than 40% of their students who enter high school in the freshman year. The systemic cause of most of the drop out issues, among boys, is the goals that school districts, states, and the US Department of Education place on instruction. There is a primary focus of learning facts, figures, and instructional pieces as the number one priority. By the time most students walk across the commencement stage at 18 years old, they have forgotten about 95% of these facts that drive our educational institutions. The correct priority should be the social and emotional development for students as they work their way through the primary and middle school grades; instructional goals should be second.

Changing the Educational Mission

When you browse the websites of the many school districts around the US, somewhere you will find the school district's important mission statement. Mission statements will focus on important cultural adaptations such as understanding diversity, success in the real world, along with school safety and social-emotional health. All of these important American values are consistently woven into most school mission statements. Below are three sample school mission statements that incorporate social-emotional health.

School I

The School District of Baraboo is dedicated to being the best educational community by supporting the maximum growth of each student, enabling each to succeed in and contribute positively to a continuously evolving world.

SCHOOL DISTRICT OF BARABOO CORE BELIEFS

- We believe education is an investment in the future of our community and society.
- Educational achievement is a collaborative process engaging students, teachers, administrators, parents and the community.
- We believe each student can learn and has the right to reach his/her full potential.
- We believe every student is entitled to an education that is responsive to his/her unique needs.
- We believe that all members of the educational community have the right to feel safe: physically, emotionally and socially.

-Baraboo Board of Education, February, 2011

School II

Greendale Schools | **Mission Statement**

The Greendale School District, in partnership with students, families, and the community, is committed to developing leadership, creativity, and educational excellence. By creating multiple opportunities for learning, each student's unique abilities are developed to achieve success and contribute positively to our global society.

Belief Statements

- Children must be prepared for the future.
- All children can learn.
- A high quality public education includes a broad range of experiences for Social, physical, emotional, intellectual and creative development.
- Connecting knowledge, ideas and experiences is essential to learning.
- We are members of a global society. The awareness and understanding of this Diversity enriches us.
- Lifelong learning is necessary to the success and wellbeing of all.
- Families provide the foundations for learning and have a significant continuing role in their children's education.
- Educating children is everyone's responsibility.
- Effective communication is vital to the educational process.
- Participation of informed and educated citizens is essential to the success of our society.
- Understanding and collaborating with others are essential for success.
- People are our most valuable resource.
- Every person has value, is unique and deserves respect and dignity.
- Everyone has a right to a safe environment.

School III

Rockford Public Schools Mission Statement

The mission of the Rockford Public School District is to provide the teaching and learning environments which will ensure, with the support of the students, parents and community, that all students, upon graduation, will have the academic and social skills and strategies to be successful life-long learners.

Before these lasting mission statements, found in these important school districts, is where the values stop. The incredible missing link is that the mission statements suggest the educational goal is success in the real world. However, if you follow the curriculum lessons of a fifth grade teacher, you will find no lesson plans or orientation on social-emotional goals. Rather, the entire school day is based on instructional goals. Nothing is found on problem solving, conflict resolution, identity crisis, and gender roles for boys and girls. With federal laws such as NCLB, and state accountability standards, these important American values are nowhere to be found in today's classroom. In the three listed mission statements there is nothing to indicate that all students will graduate, it is just assumed that many students will drop out. The most important educational mission of any K-12 school system is the completion of educational status that ends with high school graduation. Failure to include the graduation issue in the mission statement is a tragic instructional oversight.

In the past, we have put great stock in the schools to solve American problems and issues. We have Title I funds to help students who are lower income with free and reduced lunch. We have homeland security grants, and other important pieces to place money in school to tell students not to use drugs and to value proper eating through lunch programs. This long history of entrusting public schools to solve cultural issues has been happening for decades. Yet the dropout crisis for boys is absolutely phenomenal and nowhere do we have intervention plans to help these boys correct their behavior. Instead, we let them drop out and become perpetrators or victims of crime and other illicit activities. Their chances of adequate employment are poor, and they lack the necessary values that might prevent them from performing bad behavior. The trend of boy dropouts is getting larger and larger with each passing day. Today, in the state of Michigan, as you read this book, in five hours or less, approximately 55 boys will drop out of high school. Still we march on with our instructional goals and do nothing to prevent these tragic events.

High School Graduation Crisis

In the world of high school many boys just fail to connect with adults and the academic requirements mandated by states and local school districts. Most of these males will not return to high school or receive further education. Their chances of getting gainful employment and moving forward in the 21st century are weak. High schools around the US do not address this problem (the retention of boys in high school) with any sort of serious, systematic approach. Once a student falls behind in the curriculum, their grades suffer, self-esteem lowers, and they are simply lost and forgotten. After 2001, "No Child Left Behind" looked at greater accountability standards for high school students. This push towards academic rigor and over-emphasis on test scores exacerbated the dropout problem. School administrators, personnel and teachers were pressured to raise test scores for all students. Although this is a noble cause, it simply pushed the at-risk students and students with lower test scores right out the door. Since most at-risk students produce poor test scores, there was an unintentional consequence of systematically seeing them leave high schools. When a poor test score walks out the door as a dropout taking along sometimes perplexing behaviors it, in effect, helps the test performance. This is a backwards and very illogical approach to helping high school students. As a matter of fact, under "No Child Left Behind," we have caused a greater burden to our American culture. There is now a whole generation of males who have been pushed out of high schools because of their weak academic performance.

National Graduation Rates for Boys

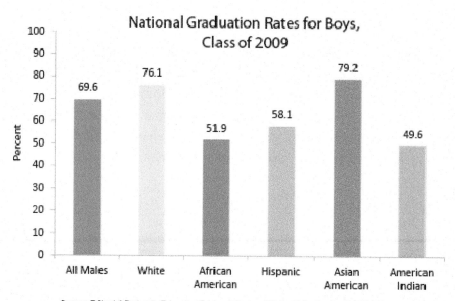

Source: Editorial Project in Education Research Center, "National Graduation Brief 2012," special supplement to Education Week's Diplomas Count 2012.

Some will go back and get their GED and some will go to vocational schools, but the majority will never return to school. Most of these males that choose not to return to school end up engaging in risky behavior that puts them in conflict with American cultural values and most end up in the Department of Corrections. A number of high schools, in a John Hopkins study in 2006, were labeled "Dropout Factories." Some of these high schools graduate less than 30% of their students. When we apply this statistic to a business analogy, producing TV sets, if only 70% are functional at the end of the line, we will see that we have grossly failed in helping students achieve a basic but necessary asset in American culture – a high school diploma. Propagated further by "No Child Left Behind" the serious lack of accountability behind middle and high school walls to prevent kids from dropping out allows the cycle to continually repeat itself.

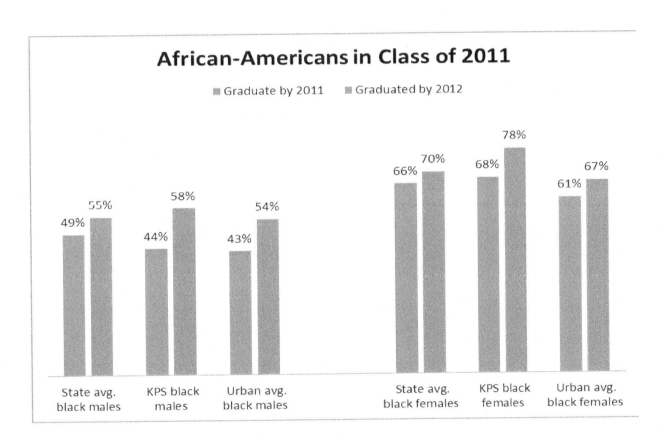

(**Source:** Michigan Center for Educational Performance & Information, 2012, State of Michigan 2012 Cohort Four-Year, 2011 Cohort Five-Year and 2010 Six-Year Graduation and Dropout Rate including Subgroups, 2013)

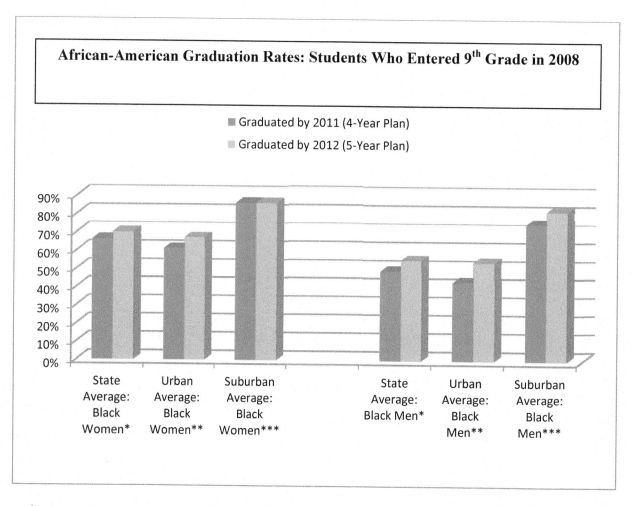

African-American Graduation Rates: Students Who Entered 9th Grade in 2008

- Graduated by 2011 (4-Year Plan)
- Graduated by 2012 (5-Year Plan)

Categories (left to right):
State Average: Black Women*, Urban Average: Black Women**, Suburban Average: Black Women***, State Average: Black Men*, Urban Average: Black Men**, Suburban Average: Black Men***

(**Source:** Michigan Center for Educational Performance & Information, 2012, *State of Michigan 2012 Cohort Four-Year, 2011 Cohort Five-Year and 2010 Six-Year Graduation and Dropout Rate including Subgroups*, 2013)

* State Average is based on the overall graduation rate of all African-American women, in all public school districts, across the State of Michigan.

** Urban Average is based on the random selection of 7 school districts across the State of Michigan; Battle Creek, Flint, Grand Rapids, Jackson, Lansing, Muskegon and Saginaw.

***Suburban Average is based on the random selection of 7 school districts across the State of Michigan; Grosse Pointe, Troy, East Lansing, East Grand Rapids, Birmingham, Ann Arbor and Bloomfield Hills.

Armed Services Qualifications and High School Dropouts

For decades, students who dropped out of high school at the early age of 14, 15 and 16 could find their way to the armed services. However, as technology increased in military applications and weaponry, all branches of the armed services decided, in 2003, that students without a high school diploma would NOT be eligible for military service careers. Therefore, anyone who signed up for the Army had to have a high school diploma and take an entrance test called the Armed Forces Vocational Aptitude Battery (ASVAB) to qualify for a changing 21st century military. This was true for the Army, Navy, Marines, Coast Guard and Air Force. For instance, the Coast Guard has the highest required ASVAB score at 40 and the Army has the lowest qualifying score at 31. Other branches of service, like the Air Force, require a minimum score of 36, the Marines-32 and the Navy-35.

Past high school dropouts used to show up at the recruiters office and find a job in an enlistment package with one of the branches of the armed service. This is no longer the case. Rather, students that graduate with a weak GPA 1.8-2.2, even with a high school diploma, may not even qualify to enter the armed forces. Now, the students who want to become part of the military are our C+/B- students who can perform well on standardized tests and earn a high school diploma. The boys who drop out have no opportunities in the very helpful and structured environment that the armed services can provide.

Chapter 4: The Warlock Gene

Almost all boys growing up today have the "warlock gene." Although this is hardly a scientific notation or a properly identified, biological gene pool, most boys have a need to dominate, seek power and take control. For whatever reason this inherent need within boys' biological systems often manifests in school settings. Boys have to seek status, power, and control. With their fragile egos and need to seek this power, boys often find themselves in numerous ego conflicts. With loads of energy, tons of enthusiasm, and the need to seek power and control, it is no wonder that we have so many personality conflicts between boys in schools.

Although strong school structure, support, and discipline can help keep some of the warlock gene in check, boys still need an adequate and appropriate channel to exert this enthusiasm, machismo, domination, and need for control. When left unchecked, this manifests itself in the form of things like bullying, school gangs, and other informal and unsupervised groups that create hardships and conflict within schools.

Mass Media Influences

All of this need for power and control is reinforced through many of the images boys find in mass media. Whether it's seen in video games full of warfare, guns, violence, action, and killing, or it's on TV, in action packed movies, images of this domination and control are reinforced daily. Additionally, all the past historical events including all of the hundreds and thousands of wars that have existed also reinforce the need for territoriality, power, and control. Although there is much to be learned from the study of history and social studies, these images leave important "imprints" on males and their conceptual roles in society.

Competition vs. Cooperative Support

Within the K-12 school structure we will find many important pieces where competition is reinforced. The pursuit of things like good grades, athletic achievements, and being in the top reading group all reinforce competition within the walls of a school. Schools seldom say that they encourage competition between students on the basis of their intellectual ability, but one of a school's primary missions is to sort and separate kids. Those that fall on the bottom portion struggle to find their niche within the school walls, especially as they reach the upper grades. While this competitive part of school can be good, it reinforces the pieces of our great American culture. Rarely do we provide cooperation or assistance for those students who fall on the bottom part of the competition ladder. When a male student reaches 5th or 6th grade it is often discovered that he is struggling academically due to improper reading and comprehension scores, inabilities to process information, or weak math computation skills. At this point, a student's ability to catch up is often overwhelming. It takes massive interventions to have a student catch up when writing, reading, and math abilities suffer at an early age.

Schools need to change their way of doing business. For years we've created a problem with boys by allowing some boys to gain power over others. Boys who fail to seek power through self-esteem, academic achievement, or extra-curricular achievement, fall by the wayside, suffer, drop out of high school, and become great burdens on society. We need to change if we want to help students find their warlock gene and appropriately channel it. Currently, the only appropriate mechanism in American society is our public school system. Our foremost challenge is to find ways for boys to channel their need to fight, seek power, and dominate. This can be done through several avenues, namely recreation, leisure, sports, and other appropriate motor activities.

Bully Behavior and Warlock Manifestation

Larry was one of the meanest bullies at my middle school. He had a whole network of friends and would pick on kids that were frail, shy and had low self-esteem. They were easy targets for Larry. Larry had a difficult upbringing with a highly dominant mother and an abusive father who left home when he was about 6 years old. Larry's academic performance was weak and his reading ability was poor. He decided to make a living stroking his ego (warlock gene needs) by picking on vulnerable kids in the unstructured time of school. I was aware of this and kept a special eye on Larry. However, other kids were often afraid to make comments about being bullied by Larry due to fear of retaliation. I had a number of conferences with Larry and his mother, but it was clear they were both in denial. Therefore, I decided to take on a new approach. In January of Larry's 8th grade year I decided to issue a Bully Survey of all 8th graders. At the end of the survey, under strict confidentiality, the last question on the survey was to please write down 1, 2 or 3 bullies in the school. In the 8th grade class of 405 students, Larry's name appeared on 256 surveys. Following the survey I had another meeting with Larry and his mom where I expressed my concerns and let them both know that this was a serious problem that needed a solution. I recommended counseling services for the two of them, but of course Larry's warlock gene interfered and he was unable to admit that there was a problem. Since they refused to go to counseling the problems with Larry did not get any better. In mid-February of his 8th grade year he was denied all lunch privileges. He would eat lunch in the office while I was out doing hall duty. Mom and Larry both did not like this, but my goal was for Larry to understand his reading disability, which he masked with bully behavior. After 6 weeks of eating lunch in the office, Larry finally agreed to start seeing a counselor after school; paid for and provided by the district. Slowly, by the end of Larry's 8th grade year, his Warlock Gene subsided to a degree where his bully behavior was reduced dramatically. As Larry entered high school he began to have frequent run-ins with the police and was caught in the act of several small robberies. Because of his persistent delinquent behavior, Larry ended up in Children's Village (a juvenile jail). At this point, Larry finally asked for more counseling. He went on to re-enter high school, stopped bullying, and earned his high school degree. After high school Larry decided that he worked better when he was alone and not in a group. He began a career as a long distance truck driver and has been successful ever since. Recently, he found my email, contacted me, and formally apologized for being a bully in the 8th grade. He accepted the fact that he must have hurt a lot of kids' feelings and knew that he bullied many students. Larry is a perfect example of how the unscientific trait that I call the "warlock gene," the need to dominate and control, can often interfere with good academic progress.

Chapter 5: Disengaged Dad's Disorder (DDD)

Disengaged Dads: A National Crisis

We've heard it too many times; "It's difficult being a dad." Confusing role models and cultural bias against dads make it a truly tough job to be fully engaged with our sons. When we look at family issues like divorce and observe the way that many Friend of the Court systems work, we see an obvious bias towards mothers. Boys, 80-90% of the time, end up in the custody of their mothers. Additionally, in most school systems, when a student is in trouble or when there is a need to contact home, the principal, assistant principal, or teacher says, "I'm going to call your mother about this." Or when there is an emergency or need to call home, it's always the first inclination to call the mother. This conceptual framework works against dads, being engaged both in schools and in the lives of their sons. For boys with disengaged or disappeared dads, this leaves a lifelong emotional scar. Generally, the boys that have disengaged, disappeared dads are much more likely to end up in trouble at school, or drop out altogether. The high school dropout rate is eight times higher for boys than girls and almost 20 times higher for boys who have disengaged fathers. As a result, we have a whole school culture of boys who are "father hungry".

The Fatherless Cycle Continues

For many fathers, being engaged is difficult because they may have missed that same parenting from their own fathers and so the cycle continues, generation after generation. It really is hard being a dad because many fathers are unable to engage because of things like huge employment responsibilities, divorces, or other important issues. When dads are absent, boys become father hungry and are more likely to be depressed, fall into delinquency, violence, crime, and develop self-esteem issues. They also struggle with emotional commitments with friends, peers, and girlfriends. If we look at the attendance at things like parent teacher conferences, we will find that the ratio of who shows up almost four to one, moms to dads. With special education students, it's higher. Moms disproportionately (probably closer to 8:1) attend Individualized Education Planning committee meetings for special ed. students. The disengagement piece of fathers is a major cause of poor school performance for boys. Schools seldom sponsor events that encourage familial relationships just for dads. Only occasionally you will find schools that do things like "Donuts with Dads" in the morning to encourage father-son relationships or "Dad's Night Out" with boys at a local recreation activity. Often, other male teachers are recruited to fill in for those boys that can't come with their own father.

The Myth of the Macho Father

Boys need the connectedness with their father or father figure. This need is expressed much differently by girls. The connectedness for dads is not through being rough and tough, but through activity, sports, and body motion. For instance, one of the best ways that boys communicate with their dads, especially those between the ages of 2 and 12, is wrestling on the living room floor. This is a way that boys show affection to their father, is a good way to release pent up energy, and just have fun. It keeps the boys moving and allows for a strong bond between father and son. It also helps to regulate the warlock gene. This type of bonding is immensely important for boys. Fun, wrestling, types of activities can lead to lifelong engagements with dad if done on a regular basis. Boys will look forward to wrestling with dad every single day if given the opportunity. The father himself is caught between the code of being a boy or a tough man displaying a macho image. We see this throughout all of mass media, the sports on TV, and the importance of being physically strong and macho. These messages are wrong and confusing for boys. It is important for boys to understand emotional attachment, show feelings, and even cry. Society's rigor on machismo creates confusing and perplexing messages for boys. They do not know the proper way to show these types of emotional pieces. Certainly, one thing that allows boys to partake in a wide-range of emotions is participation in athletics and sports. Without sports as a forum for alleviating motion and establishing a bond with father, boys are often straight-jacketed by the emotionalism of our culture. Instead of machismo, fathers need to connect emotionally with their sons. Sometimes talking eye-to-eye is too confrontational for boys but activities such as going for a walk and walking side-by-side outdoors can establish meaningful and important bonds with sons. Leisure and recreation activities, along with sports, are a huge bonding agent between fathers and sons.

Moms Marketplace Message in Schools (MMM)

The next time you walk into an elementary school, take a minute to determine who the classroom assistant is; odds are that it's going to be a mom. The homeroom coordinator or the parent who helps the teacher is almost invariably a mother. Although these things are important for moms to be involved with, there is such a thing as an overabundance of female influence in schools. Such overabundance offers boys with fewer role models and provides even fewer interactions with older males. If we look at the rosters of para-pros and teacher assistants across the country they are overwhelmingly female. Boys read these messages, and develop an over-reliance on female teachers as the whole elementary experience becomes saturated with women. As a result, we create a perfect storm. Dads become invariably disengaged with their sons and the school systems that are oversaturated with females. As it is, boys hardly stand a chance at finding male role models in their first seven years of public school education, an unintended consequence of early education that has created a huge disadvantage and a form of discrimination against boys. If the public school system continues to operate at its current rate, then boys' dropout incidences, self-esteem issues and perplexity towards violence will continue to grow with each passing year. Certainly, fathers hold a great amount of responsibility for not engaging in and being a part of their children's elementary school years. There are ample opportunities and experiences available for dads. Unless the status quo changes boys will continue to go forward without ever having the opportunity to question this experience and feel the benefit of a fully engaged father.

Grading Mom and Dad

Educators spend a lot of time teaching kids within the structure of a relatively short school day and most parents do their best to send their kids to school, well prepared, each day. However, some parents do not meet the necessary qualifications and do not adequately prepare their children to attend class. Poor parenting can come in the form of a lack of clean clothes, inappropriate lunches or no money for lunch, enabling children to stay up late, and other unproductive behavior. Kids will often talk about their home life at school and most teachers are quick to figure out what happens at home. They hear the stories of emotional abuse and sometimes physical abuse that occurs within the confines of a home. Many students have difficult living environments and reasonable support systems (i.e. lack of access to technology and transportation for extracurricular involvement).

Therefore, it seems only fair that each teacher grade both mom and dad and student since doing well in school is a students' and parents' responsibility. Accountability could be increased if parents were given grades on each report card. This rubric would include items such as, supportive home environment, appropriate support systems, access to technology, and parental involvements in school. In fact, an exhaustive list of factors could be evaluated and graded by teachers. This would give mom and dad feedback in how they are doing. Parents today are not meeting their responsibilities. Whether it's because they had one too many beers the night before or simply because they're generally disinterested, it might act as a wakeup call for parents to help their son or daughter to be successful in school if we provide the necessary evaluations of parenting practices. Many parents do not provide a supportive home environment and place very little emphasis on school and the skills needed to be successful during the school day. Parents' failures to provide stability at home can ultimately result in a student becoming a high school dropout.

Chapter 6: Adolescence is Not Adolescence

From the onset of puberty to age 19, boys are discovering the world that is their bodies. Their minds are preoccupied with body and hormonal growth. They run the orientation back and forth between physical wants and desires, understanding athleticism, and sexual wants and desires. This important process of their growth, from age 11-19, is about body development, not about social-emotional growth. Although their social-emotional growth does develop during this time period, their primary preoccupation is with their bodies. Their entire life patterns and orientation will be established during this time period. They will sort and select themselves on the basis of strength, height, weight, and other kinesthetic activities. Similarly, the world of employment will be based on three primary strains. Students will seek and take employment on the basis of body back, body hands, and body brain. In other words, they will take on the body back when they use their body as a function during more labor intensive work. For those who focus on more technical degrees, they will end up using body hands. For those who end up with white collar degrees, they will use body mind. Notice the absence in all this is of social-emotional development. Social-emotional development happens much later in life. For most young males this will occur at a level of complete maturation, 30 to 50 years old. For some, more self-actualized social-emotional growth might happen during later stages of life. Our society reinforces the use of the body and many young adolescent boys, who have the warlock gene, are tempted to conquer and only understand the need for power, body motion, and control. For instance, there is little encouragement and reinforcement for boys who are more empathetic and sensitive to pursue careers in caring industries like elementary education, nursing and medical assistance; industries that are overwhelmingly dominated by women. We often question any male who decides to pursue this line of work. For instance, when a male says he wants to be a kindergarten teacher, the first thing that comes to our society's mind is "he must be gay". These stereotypes reinforce much of this body back and hands orientation for boys. Systematically around the US, there is a decline in male elementary teachers and the number of men entering the caring profession of nursing has essentially flat lined.

Sexually, boys are often on the prowl to conquer as many females as possible. Their dominance-controlled sexual urges make this a matter of supremacy, warlock needs, and domination. Social-emotional connections between male and female are often very limited at this adolescent age. Boys are chasing females based on sexual needs and urges. Adolescent, physical and sexual urges are often overwhelming and predominant for males. These urges and needs are all-consuming and often alter all sorts of behavior in a boy's attempt to solicit females. Boys do not have the social-emotional development or mental capacity to make strong emotional connections with girls in the early adolescent years, it is simply about conquest. These pieces are reinforced by mass media, and other visual imagery which portray many mixed, sexual messages for boys.

Revealing clothing and physical appearance of females continues to regulate male behavior. If one steps back and looks at changes in adolescence dating rituals, it is clear that relationships are even less permanent now in the 21st century than they were in the 50s, 60s, and 70s. For a boy and girl to have a long-term relationship, for a year or more, is nearly unheard of by today's dating standards. This important topic that we call "love," for boys, is based on superficial parts of relationships such as looks, dress, attire and sexuality on behalf of the female. Strong emotional connectedness does not occur until much later in life. Schools fail to realize this important piece and do not understand these relationships between boys and girls. Things are often very temporary and girls can set off signals that reveal superficial sexual attractiveness. For boys, the most important emotional bonds, often woven into important athletic pieces, are long-term relationships with other boys through team oriented sports. These emotional bonds with players on the team, best friends who share physical activity, will be much deeper and more meaningful than relationships with females. The athletic, game-oriented, regulations of how to express emotions and how to develop relationships are laid out more clearly for boys in sports than they are in random dating patterns between boys and girls in middle school and high school. This need for structure and rules, which is satisfied in the confines of team sports, is much easier for boys to manage. Unfortunately our society gives many mixed messages on what is right and wrong outside of formal athletic relationships. Unfortunately in our schools and society, we attempt to treat boys, as they approach the age of maturity, as full grown, mature, emotional adults, when in reality, they are just beginning the developmental phase of their lives.

Boys and Emotional Connections at School

Some of the greatest experiences for boys at school take place when they make an emotional connection with an adult. This can be their favorite teacher or the coach or instructor of an extracurricular activity. Once the student has broken through this difficult barrier, one that can be challenging for a lot of boys, the emotional connection is a permanent hook. If boys can make an emotional connection with just one adult in school, then everything changes. When boys make an emotional bond with another male or female teacher they turn school from a chore to an adventure. Once school becomes an adventure through this strong relationship, boys will utilize that relationship to discount their "warlock gene" needs. Emotional relationships at school enable boys to enjoy themselves and become highly productive in conjunction with their adult mentor's support.

Chapter 7 – Lessons and Resilience: Facing Setbacks

The public education system in the United States is one of the great staples of the American way of life. It is the foundation of many opportunities and choices for all sorts of young Americans. As a professor at Eastern Michigan University, I am reflecting on my twelve years of college and nowhere in my recollection do I recall taking a class in gender training; nor will our up-and-coming teachers. The basis of a new teacher's experience and training on the differences between boys and girls is left to serendipity. As a matter of fact, most new teachers can articulate very little in the differences of gender approaches. This leaves a serious deficit in delivery of lessons, learning activities, and mainstream objectives. Rather the focus of their education has been on curriculum, classroom instruction and behavior management. The behavior management pieces are given to beginning teachers on a gender neutral basis. As a result of the education of more and more female (and fewer and fewer male) teachers, the occurrences of boy failures, happening at early grades, continues to grow as this pattern spreads. My own son went through eight years in a public school before he ever had a male teacher. Girls invariably do better, all through K-12, as a function of their ability to cope with resilience. Boys can go to elementary school for seven years and NEVER have a male teacher. This makes very little sense.

Schools' Silent Objectives: Sorting and Selecting of Students

One of the major difficulties of working with boys in our K-12 system is the willingness of schools to **sort and select** students so quickly. The sorting of students is a demonstration of our focus on competition as a reflection of American society but our focus on competition, sorting, and selecting of students is premature. In many ways sorting and selecting students is part of a school's unstated mission. Some examples are:

- Grades
- Honors and Awards
- Assessment tests
- Special Health Classes
- Special Education
- Gifted and Talented Programs
- Remedial Programs
- Honors Classes
- G.P.A. Class Rank
- Selection of Athletic Teams
- National Honor Society

This list is not meant to be comprehensive and could include many other types of school activities.

Certainly, the competitive part of school, for students, is getting ready for admission to a post high school institution. However, the sorting and selecting of students often happens with great vitality, especially in the early grades where it can damage fragile boys' egos. In addition, we put little emphases on helping boys to cope with resistance and setbacks. In elementary schools, we place students in pods, a relatively new educational technique. As they sit in groups of three to six, with the tables pushed together, students are asked to cooperate and work together, yet all of their assessments are done on an individual basis. Little time in the elementary grades is spent in a cooperative setting with students working together to help each other. This mixed message poses big problems for boys. We have discovered that when boys get poor grades on tests their egos may suffer, disproportionately, because they have not been taught appropriate coping skills. This is unfortunate because, when delivered properly, a poor grade on a test in the fourth grade actually could be a very positive experience. The ability to overcome setbacks and other negative issues is an important part of the resilience that is not taught in K-12 schools. Boys who feel the need to dominate and control must learn appropriate coping skills when they cannot win, dominate or control. Many boys who do not learn coping skills often get labeled and placed in special categories (e.g. Emotional Impairment) due to their lack of problem solving skills in the face of setbacks.

Schools need to quickly identify the kids who are on the bottom end of the selection process. These are the kids with low GPAs and low self-esteem. These students are self-conscious because they are not performing at satisfactory, school-determined, levels. Nobody knows this more than the students themselves. When boys are handed a geometry tests that has a big "F" on it, this hurts their pride, ego, and diminishes their feelings of worth in the school. For many boys it's a lot easier to just withdraw and drop out rather than face these instructional challenges. Schools do not go out and identify these at risk students or develop intervention plans specifically for them. I believe that all students with a cumulative GPA under a 2.0 should have an intervention plan that will assist them in overcoming their academic challenges. Boys need to be told that they are not failures because they got an "F" on a geometry test. This needs to be reinforced by someone who the boy respects; boys need help and emotional support in overcoming these academic struggles. Without outside intervention and emotional support surely these students will drop out of school and take on a low paying, dead-end job.

Attention Deficit/Hyperactivity Disorder (A. D. H . D)

One of the greatest American tragedies is the number of boys who go through the K-12 public school system labeled as ADD or ADHD. Most of the staff doing the labeling are female and about 80% of students diagnosed with ADHD are boys. This tragedy stems from the fact that boys want to be active, they want to move, they want to exercise their body and be in motion. Yet school is a place where they must sit in a seat, remain quiet, and listen to auditory delivery systems. This works in direct conflict with the biological programming of boys during their grade school and middle school years. At that age, most boys haven't developed the internal controls to remain quiet and sit still when their biological system is screaming at them to do just the opposite. There is little sympathy or empathy for these types of active boys. Rather, the immediate response from most professionals is to consider medication and designation as ADD or ADHD. Ritalin, and other behavior modification drugs are a much easier approach than modifying a teacher's delivery system. It is no coincidence that the number of boys diagnosed with ADHD has gone up as the number of male teachers in elementary schools has decreased. Through the use and over-use of drugs like Ritalin, we have created an easy fix for hundreds of thousands of boys. Giving them medication, as opposed to teaching them the proper instructional techniques and allowing them to move, exercise, and participate in kinesthetic activities in the classroom, is counterproductive to their natural development. The third grade is the most typical year when teachers start to make the recommendation for ADHD testing and medication. In the growth of my own three boys, all three of their third grade teachers recommended medication because of their hyperactivity. For parents who cannot stand up to teachers, any suggestion that a child has ADD or ADHD can be shocking and overwhelming. As a corollary, all three of my boys are "A" students and have gone on to do phenomenal things in education without any type of medication. Teachers in our K-12 system simply need to come to the realization that boys' internal controls are going to develop later than their physical movement needs. And yet nowhere in the development and education of new teachers do we teach this necessary piece of putting active motion into the classroom each and every class period. From now until the sun stops shining, we're going to have active boys in classrooms who are going to need to exercise. Simply asking the boys to sit still, be quiet, and keep their mouths closed is an impossible proposition. It is simply not realistic to expect such behavior from all boys. Any lofty expectations to the contrary will create a huge emotional disconnect between boys and teachers (mostly female) where boys feel out of place, without answers, and their self-esteem is often crushed.

The forging of relationships in American public schools is a very important piece of social-emotional development that boys experience while attending school. Different from their female counterparts, whose relationships are often bonded by the sharing of experiences and emotions,

34

boys bond in relationships within a totally different framework. This framework is often the sharing of what I refer to as an "external bond." These external bonds are based on some form of activity or motor movement that boys share. Due to the influence of mass media, these relationship pieces are very important to boys, but they often lack the skills to initiate, sustain, and maintain these relationships. Some of the relationships that boys have while growing up are based on direction from their parents. These are based on decisions concerning the types of activities that boys will participate in outside of school, such as extra-curricular activities, sports, or clubs. When boys come home from school and parents ask about their day, more often than not, they will tell their parents what they did at school, generally out on the playground, not what they learned or encountered. Boys maintain relationships with each other through two primary mechanisms; the redirection of the warlock gene, and/or physical, motor activity. In the manner of engaging their ego, boys often find appropriate or inappropriate ways of channeling their warlock gene. Recently, I was talking to a group of former students who made a living of bullying people in the middle school. They, of course, picked on kids who were smaller, fragile emotionally and weak physically. This group of bullies saw the weaker kids as targets and would bond by picking on them. This taunting, which happened in the unstructured time at school, particularly on the bus, created a bond between these two strong, bullying types of kids. At the time, I asked them why they thought they bullied. They said that they were bored, but they probably suffered from low self-esteem. Now that they are older and their emotional intelligence has matured, they say that it was wrong and they shouldn't have done it. Their inappropriate verbal remarks and physical pushing, shoving, poking, teasing and taunting created a bond between the two boys. It was a game of one-upmanship for their egos to see who could make their victim cry first. On the larger scale, it should be noted that the two bullies had trouble surviving through high school. They barely graduated, and both have low-paying service-sector jobs. Their victim now has a master's degree and makes a successful living in the computer technology area. Sometimes boys will actually bond with the appropriate use of redirection of the warlock gene in a helping mode. For instance, boys who are student leaders will bond because they hold elected, student council positions or other pieces meant to help with human services at school. Working for a cause, raising money, or helping with SADD are ways that these boys can do positive things and create bonds in appropriate ways. Generally these are for the more mature and high self-esteemed boys who choose the path of helping others less fortunate than themselves. However, it all falls back on the need, of most boys, to be in power, have control, and dominate situations. Only a small, select group of kids are capable of collaborating maturely in middle and high school. These boys are the exceptions, not the rule.

Chapter 8: Magic of Movement

Boys need to be active, exercise and move every day. Ability to move can solve many of the warlock gene issues. Within the walls of schools, every student should partake in an extra-curricular activity every semester. All students need to be involved in school and find a niche. For those boys who have yet to find their identity or fall on the lower part of the domination ladder, finding a niche is going to be their salvation. Whether this is through athletics, participating in the bowling club, the robotics club, or being the best mechanic in the school, all boys need regular movement every day. Unfortunately, taking directions from "No Child Left Behind," auditory delivery of instruction has increased "still time" for boys. All students are asked to sit longer in their seat and listen to rather long and boring pieces of auditory forms of instruction. In public education, the use of kinesthetic forms of learning has been on the decline for many years. One way to enrich kinesthetic education is to mandate extra movement activities each and every day. Many countries in the Pacific Rim have mandatory kinesthetic and exercise for all students in the morning and afternoon. In addition, we have eliminated recess in nearly all elementary schools, as it no longer counts as instruction time. This has been one of the biggest and most profound mistakes in the history of public education. Denying active and over-active boys the opportunity to get out and move on the playground, where they exert their energy, have fun with friends and play informal games, has caused further alienation of those boys in need of physical release. All boys need regular movement and at least 60 minutes of vigorous exercise per day. This would go a long way in solving many of the frustrations that boys encounter while sitting through long classes each school day. The need for rigorous movement aside, helping boys conquer their "warlock gene" issues through competitive sports is a very important part of growing up.

All boys need to be part of a competitive, athletic experience because it is in the athletic arena that they learn to deal with many of their emotions. Is it okay to be sad? Is it okay to celebrate? Is it okay to show affection after an important achievement? In addition, boys learn how to win and also, more importantly, how to lose. One of the greatest gifts we can give to boys, in the development of their pre-adolescent and adolescent years, is a competitive sport experience. For some boys, it is necessary for them to be part of a competitive sport through all their developmental years. Boys that have this competitive experience are better adjusted, can find appropriate ways to channel their "warlock gene" issues, and can deal, appropriately, with emotions and feelings on a daily basis. The athletic experience is perhaps the only important part of development and growth where we teach boys to shift emotional gears. It's okay to jump up and down with joy and it's okay to be sad. This is easily learned through the celebration of athletic achievements, and failures.

Religion of Sport

Many boys' problems and concerns can be effectively addressed through body motion. The most important single task we can provide our boys is regular physical activity, six days a week.

Our greatest gift, during their growth years, is providing an outlet for exercise on a regular basis. This not only helps them cope with many of the anxieties that they face, but also allows them to displace "warlock gene" issues by providing cognitive and intellectual function and support. Everything from hyperactivity disorders to anxieties and emotional impairment issues can be solved with a large dose of regular and active exercise. Unfortunately, our schools are providing just the opposite. The NCLB movement has systematically eliminated the most important educational component, school recess. Back when I went to elementary school, we enjoyed the benefits of a morning recess, a lunch time recess, and an afternoon recess. For most boys, this covered our 60 minute per day, full body motion requirements.

What Has Happened to Elementary Recess?

Throughout the late 1990s and early 2000s, we put tremendous efforts into increased accountability via state test scores under NCLB. Many states moved away from the number of "instructional days" model to the number of "instructional hours per day" model. Under the new model, passing time, lunch and recess do not count as instructional time. To meet the rigorous demands of NCLB, state accountability, and testing procedures, recesses were eliminated in an effort to raise test scores. This ill-conceived logic did not systematically raise test scores. Instead, we are now discriminating against elementary students, particularly boys. We ask third graders to remain seated, hearing mostly auditory types of instruction, from 8:50am-12:10pm. If you were to ask any adult to do that, it would nearly be impossible. For those boys who can't sit still, we categorize them ADHD or label them with some other anxiety disorder and attempt to manipulate their internal need to move around. NCLB was designed as a well-intended conceptual framework to help with teacher accountability. It has, in fact, created greater hardships for boys, alienated them from academic success, placed them farther behind their counterparts, and caused a great divide between male and female achievement. Most of the boys who suffer the fallout go on to drop out of high school. If we examine a Tuesday afternoon in the local city where houses are close together, we do not see students outside on the streets. Playing hockey, basketball, running around, and playing various kid games is essentially a thing of the past. If you drive by the bus stop on any afternoon, you will see a parade of parents' cars lined up to get their children because they are afraid to let them walk home alone. This has been a major culture shift in the past decade. Today, kids rush home to get behind a piece of glass; video machines, the TV, the computer, or other types of small box entertainment. Therefore, recess and the important interactions that are accomplished during school is the only time that many children get for important body motion activity. We are hindering students' abilities to resolve important issues in informal settings which help with social-emotional and cognitive development. Without necessary recess time, morning, afternoon and lunch, students are deprived of both their cognitive and social-emotional growth. This social-emotional growth has now been turned over to the local video store or small box game. Next time you are at the local elementary school, watch kids come in from a 20 minute recess period and watch the teacher settle them down as they switch gears, this will take as little as a minute or two. When students come in from play they are on task, they are ready to learn, they concentrate better, they sit still, and they are ready to begin their academic lesson.

We've Got it all Backwards

Somehow in the last 15 years, educators have made the decision that increased instructional time at the sacrifice of body movement and/or recess would be a good thing. They theorized that less body movement and more time on task would increase learning and help test scores. This is where the problem begins. Test scores are simply tests, arbitrary information measuring how a student processes information at one moment in time, but test scores don't equate to job performance. Test scores are also a very poor indicator of how children will survive in a place of employment with fellow colleagues and worker productivity expectations. We put millions and millions of dollars into accountability and test scores but for what great purpose? As far as helping students to become productive citizens, better people in the real world, and contributing members of the work force is concerned, there is little correlation. You see, we've got it all backwards. What students need in elementary schools is not the mandate of having to sit still for three hours in the morning and three hours in the afternoon. Children need to move, they need to get outside, solve problems, and interact with their peers during the unstructured time of their lives. This is a tremendously important part of early adolescence and elementary school development. How could we go so wrong? We have students who don't exercise after school, epidemic obesity in our country, a tragic increase of students being labeled ADHD, or LD, and yet we've taken away the most important part of the school day. Certainly academics are important, but the ability to provide consistent exercise at appropriate intervals increases cognitive skills. Doing just the opposite, the system we have now, with the elimination of recess, causes problems for boys and decreases academic readiness. We have shot ourselves in the foot and are clearly discriminating against boys. The NCLB reform has caused tremendous hardships for all students (particularly boys), teachers, and administrators. It has served no great purpose except to focus on meaningless accountability test scores with no practical merit that serve no lifelong purpose. If we are really interested in helping kids find their potential, we should mandate that, each academic year, students participate in at least one extra-curricular activity, and one mandated sport. This should be for all students after 3rd grade. If we critically look at the boys that have had problems in schools and become high school dropouts, we will find that they often become disengaged from their schools. They fail to get involved in clubs, extra-curricular activities, and sports. If we're really interested in meaningful social change then we must use extracurricular activities in K-12 schools to circumvent absentee parents by encouraging students to exercise, solve warlock gene issues, resolve conflicts appropriately, and learn how to develop different male roles. If we examine why boys drop out of school, it's often based on attitude, not necessarily achievement. It takes the proper attitude to make achievement happen. Students who have dropped out of high school, upon exit interviews, will say that often times they feel that nobody at school likes them. Or, there is some sort of emotional issue going on at home. Seldom does academic readiness come to the forefront. A student may simply lack some of the skills and basic components necessary to succeed. The character and education that these extracurricular activities bring to a student is like gold for at-risk boys in today's secondary schools. The valuable lessons about conflict resolution, working together, self-esteem, hard work, and motivation learned through sports and extracurricular activities are platinum experiences for boys.

When students look back at their high school and middle school experience and report what they've learned the most, it always revolves around a person. No one will ever remember getting an A on a Social Studies test, or a great class discussion on civil rights. Rather, students reflect on their experiences about the relationships they had with specific teachers and events. With increasing class size and demands placed on all teachers, it's difficult to establish strong relationships with students during the instructional day. The time to socialize and get to know students comes during extracurricular activities and sports at every middle and high school around America. For those boy students who find great success in American middle and high schools, there is usually a strong bond with a role model in the school. Extracurricular activities allow the student the time needed to establish such bonds. Boys who drop out of high school do not form a bond within the school walls. They have no strong relationships and feel as if they are unwanted. After-school activities allow coaches, instructors and mentors to get to know students and learn about their families. These important functions create lasting parts of the character building that is needed to be successful in today's school and post-school experiences. In addition, since most of the after school activities involve physical activity; boys are able to deal with their warlock gene issues through the magic of movement. They can exercise while they develop important character traits that help grow a healthy brain. These strong relationships will last and help to build the foundation of important reflections for success in the future. This time in a boy's life, middle and high school, is where they get a chance to learn about all aspects of social-emotional growth, learn how to exercise, move, and participate in leisure and recreation; they really are the golden developmental years of one's life. All boys need the opportunity to experience body motion activities. Sports are by far the best teacher in our secondary schools.

When I was principal of a middle school, I asked the track coach to take two important emotionally impaired boys on the track team. One of the boys had an oral-compulsive problem and often didn't know how to keep his mouth closed. He was an agitator with a difficult home life and often was the source of verbal sparring issues, particularly with other boys. He had few friends, but seemed to get in everyone else's business. It was my belief that if we could get him running track and develop a good relationship with the coach, maybe some of his behaviors would extinguish. The track coach agreed, reluctantly. I made a point to stop in after school, watch the practice and check up on both the students. One of the students was named Tommy and he was going to run the 800 and 1600 meter race in the next track meet. One of the nice things about running the 800 and 1600 is that there isn't a lot of time for talking. The track coach went out of his way to show structure to Tommy and to reach out to him with positive encouragement. With a little prodding from me, the track coach quickly learned that if we could put Tommy in long runs he didn't really have a chance to talk and get into conflicts with other peers. The track coach continued to use positive reinforcement for Tommy as he improved his running skills. Soon Tommy started to place well in his races. The track coach then moved him to the 2 mile race, which seemed to be a favorite of Tommy's. In Tommy's junior year, he actually placed first in the 2 mile at a dual meet. It was a real turning point in Tommy's life when he realized that he had potential in track. Tommy was taking running much more seriously as he entered his senior year. He joined the cross country team in the fall and placed in the regional meet. He was able to develop a meaningful relationship with both the track coach and the cross country coach. His parents also noticed a positive change at home and Tommy became more disciplined and self-guided with his life. During Tommy's senior year he only had one detention for his oral compulsive problem. This was a big reduction from the 14 detentions he had in his Junior year, before he joined the track team. It is my belief that Tommy's success in track solved his oral compulsive problem and his need to dominate and irritate his peers. At the awards banquet at the end of his senior track season, his coach stated that Tommy had been one of his most famous success stories ever. A misguided kid that couldn't stop talking turned his life around for the better and became a track star.

Relationships Built Around Physical Activity

In all three grade divisions of public education, elementary, middle, and high school, when one examines physical movement, one will find boys bonding. At recess at the local elementary school, walk outside and you'll see boys playing kickball, touch football, softball, or other pick-up related games. Although they have their squabbles, boys use sports as a bonding method based on motor movement. This relationship piece, established in the early elementary grades, is greatly discounted by many administrators and deemed unimportant by many schools. Yet many boyhood and lifelong bonds are established at recess in the early elementary grades. This phenomenon is best described through the acronym of BBB (Boy, Body, Bonding). As boys grow up and discover their physical characteristics, limitations, and expectations, they develop these bonding pieces through physical activity. BBB is an important part of a boy's emotional and social development. As students get older and start to join sports teams or participate in extracurricular activities, BBB will become even more pronounced. Lifetime relationships will be forged by the sharing of body movement and physical activities between boys. Throughout third through fifth grade, many teachers can walk around and discover very quickly which boys have experienced BBB. Those boys who are absent of this type of exposure and experience will often become problematic students. Sadly, schools fail to intervene with any of these students. They are often left to deal with these social integration issues on their own or with their families and many boys have trouble making this adjustment. Schools need to assist boys, who are often alone, with finding their niche within school. This can be through BBB, leisure, recreation, the chess club, or an art experience. One way or another, students need to develop a strong niche where they can bond with other boys within the framework of the school.

Through the course of a given school day, when talking to parents, I found that the most important thing that they wanted for their kids was not to have good grades, but to have friends. The friendship piece is the most important part of school for parents and students alike. Friendship develops the emotional intelligence and the social integration experience necessary for survival in the employment world. I believe that these parents' priorities are correct since it is the social ability to get along with your peers that will result in a successful employment experience. Boys need to be encouraged to foster these types of relationships within the confines of the school day. Boys who are unable to develop healthy friendships do not thrive and become the school system's castaways. As castaways they are certain to have issues with teachers and staff, motivation problems, social integration deficiencies, poor grade performance, and are most likely headed towards a dropout experience. Although the school does not intend to develop castaways, it certainly does so through its inability to help these boys integrate. This is one important piece of encouraging school personnel to assist these boys in our elementary and middle schools.

College and University Enrollment for Boys

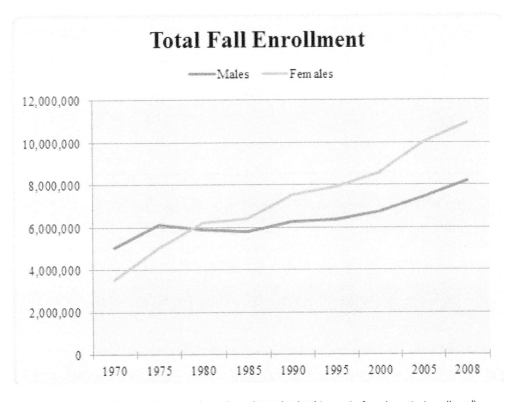

(**Source:** http://www.forbes.com/sites/ccap/2012/02/16/the-male-female-ratio-in-college/)

Chapter 9: Case Studies

James…

James was dominated by his "warlock gene" and loved to party. He was on the football team for about 2 years and this experience led him to the high school drinking scene. After an injury to his knee, which sidelined him from football, he turned his energy towards more drinking. Things got so bad during his senior year that he was drinking on a daily basis after school. On two separate occasions, at the end of his senior year, he crashed his car and was found to be intoxicated. In the second crash he did considerable property damage to a private residence when he attempted to do a shot in the drive way and lost control of the car. When he crashed his car for the 3rd time, fortunately hurting nobody but himself, he realized that he would most likely be going to jail. In the approximately 30 days he spent in jail, James dried out and realized that he needed to become alcohol free. He also had time to reflect on the best time of his life, the time when he was playing football and getting regular physical exercise. On June 19, 2000, he made a permanent commitment to stop drinking and started attending AA meetings on a regular basis. Since that time, he has remained drug and alcohol-free. James then decided to take up running since he was now 19 years old. The running helped provide structure in his life. He completed his first marathon in 2001and started completing triathlons in 2005. Most importantly he was able to start something that required movement and complete it. He would run a number of marathons, and compete in many triathlons. He even got to the point where he completed the New Zealand Ironman in 10 hours, an impressive feat for a 6 foot 3 and 185 lb man. After passing the certification test, James became a personal trainer. He continues to make triathlons and personal fitness a way of life. He is free of all his evils and has displaced his need for alcohol and drugs through the magic of movement.

Jay…

Jay was a hyperactive boy who, in 3rd grade, was diagnosed with a learning disability (LD) in writing and reading. Jay was also diagnosed with ADHD. In other words, the instruction that Jay received could not keep him in his seat. He was quick to get up, move around, and had trouble sitting still for 6 hours per day. Jay was a sensitive and sweet kid who was well liked by his peers. However, when it came to his academic performance, reading and writing, he simply could not perform. He would try to turn things in, but they would be incomplete or would lack any breath of completeness. Jay was not a discipline problem, but rather an academic burden for the school and nobody really wanted to take the time to find out what learning pieces would work for Jay. By the time he reached middle school, he was getting mostly Ds and Fs due to his inability to keep up with his peers. By the time Jay reached high school, it was obvious that he was going to be a dropout. The special ed teachers were making attempts to help him but they were making no progress. Jay had reasonable parents and, through his own vision and self-determination, wanted to go on to a post-high school educational experience. Jay did have one thing going well for him, he was athletic and a very good swimmer. This was something that his parents supported very much. Where he failed in school, he excelled in sports. Jay not only turned into an incredible swimmer, but he had a coach, a non-educator, who finally put structure in his life. His coach took the time to sit down with Jay after practices and assist him, one-on-one, with his reading issues. The coach soon found out that Jay read better backwards than forward. That he had dysgraphia problems and he worked with Jay to better process penmanship, words and thoughts. The coach organized academic lessons in the same way that one would organize a swim workout. Jay started feeling better about himself and along with his success on the swim team, his grades started to elevate to a C level. This did a number of important things for Jay. It kept him eligible for sports and allowed him to earn high school credits toward graduation. He also established a very strong bond with a male role model. This sporting activity and the magic of movement, swimming, is what propelled Jay to stay in high school all four years. Without swimming and a caring and compassionate coach, Jay would have quickly been a high school dropout. Jay went on to community college without disclosing his unique disability. His grades again suffered and he did not do well. Eventually, after working with Jay individually, I was able to get him to disclose his individualized educational planning (IEP) that helped him succeed in high school. Jay then transferred schools and has had a very successful college experience. Jay has continued to be active in sports as a way of dealing with elevating his self-esteem and assisting in brain growth and success in his life.

Appendix C-1

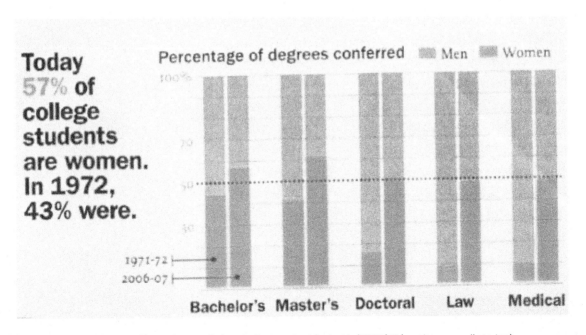

(**Source:** http://www.superscholar.org/wp-content/uploads/2010/09/gender-gap-college.jpg)

Joe...

Joe was an angry boy when he was in 8th grade. His father committed suicide when he was young and his mother seemed to have little influence or control over his behavior. His grades were mostly C's and D's in middle school and he hung around a lot of other at-risk kids. Joe did enjoy playing the drums and spent much of his free time practicing when he got a chance. Joe was not good with authority figures and rejected males that were overly dominant. During a Social Studies class, in mid-April, Joe's teacher confronted him about his inability to complete his assignments. His teacher was a middle aged, out spoken, domineering, and not terribly sensitive male. The teacher intimidated Joe, spoke to him with a raised voice, and entered Joe's personal space. After a second, similar encounter during the same week, Joe had enough. He stood up and punched his teacher with full force right square in the nose. The teacher actually fell back and hit the floor. There was a lot of blood and the teacher's nose was broken. The teacher pressed assault charges against Joe and Joe was suspended from school for the remainder of the school year. Joe was classified through the Special Education Department as an Emotionally Impaired (EI) student. When I switched from regular education to special education, Joe was my very first student. I started with Joe at the beginning of his freshman year in high school. At his IEP meeting there were many academic goals listed. There was much focus, at the time, on getting his grades back on track. As I sat at the IEP meeting with Joe and his mother, Joe was dressed in all black. He made very little eye contact and seemed withdrawn. I knew that the instructional goals were NOT what Joe needed. What Joe needed was a method to displace his anger. As a special education teacher, I started my relationship with Joe by totally ignoring the academic goals. By the second week in September, I had earned enough trust with Joe that I was able to talk him into joining me at lunch time in the weight room. Joe was relatively short and stocky and seemed like he had the body of a weight lifter. I was tall and lanky and not terribly good at weights but it didn't matter because Joe needed a place to displace his anger. After a couple weeks of joining me, almost every day, in the weight room our relationship grew. Joe started to trust me and eventually established an emotional connection with me. By December of his freshman year he was fully committed to lifting weights each day. We would rotate upper body and lower body, chest and back. By February of his freshman year, Joe had convinced his mother that joining Gold's Gym would be a good idea and he made time for longer workouts. At some point in his freshman or sophomore year, Joe came to the realization that he was successfully displacing his anger at the gym. By April of his freshman year he had gone from a small stocky kid, to a muscle bound young man. His physical transformation really helped to elevate his self-esteem. I was able to keep Joe on my caseload for his entire 4 years of high school. Soon Joe was lifting weights regularly and he no longer needed my guidance. At the start of his junior year he had changed his dress pattern and looked more like an average kid in high school. The self-discipline of the weights had also transferred to fantastic academic progress; he had elevated his grades to mostly A's and B's. At the start of his senior year, Joe made a commitment to play football for the first time in his life. Because he was so strong and small he decided to become a running back. There were many barriers that he had to overcome, including gaining the coach's trust and learning the game of football for the first tme. Joe stuck with it for the entire senior year as the 3rd string running back. He was able to play in 3 games, approximately 30 plays. After graduating, Joe applied to college and earned his B.A. degree in marketing. He continued to lift weights on a regular basis. During a reflective moment in his senior year he told me that he figured out what I did for him by making him lift weights. Joe had developed a fun personality and with his witty disposition he would add, "It was a great decision to make me start lifting weights." Three years after graduating from college Joe had a successful career working for Pitney Bowes Manufacturing Company. Soon after, Joe married a wonderful lady and they had 2 daughters. I was honored when Joe asked me to be the godparent of his girls. Joe's statement to me was real simple, "Weight lifting totally changed my life."

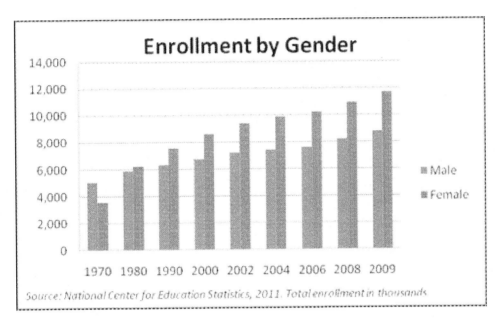

(**Source:** http://www.onlinedegrees.com/degree360/workplace/why-women-learn-more-earn-less-146.html)

Chapter 10

The Boys Solution: What Needs to Be Done

Throughout this book, I have identified a number of problems, biases, even degrees of discrimination against boys as they grow up in our K-12 systems. They are failing at a phenomenal rate, and we need to take action if we hope to save part of our great American culture. Changing the priorities of our schools will not be easy since we have not been successful in making many meaningful changes in K-12 education. We are still essentially educating kids the same way we did when the Lancaster school of delivery (1 teacher per 25 kids) was operating in the early 1920s; not much has changed since then. We've learned so much about how boys learn and their response to our current failure to teach them. They simply drop out, disappear, and cause societal problems.

I have listed 10 important steps that our schools need to take to get boys on track in K-12 education. These Action Plans give them a fighting chance to do well in post-secondary experiences, college, vocational school, and jobs. We need to teach the next generation of boys how to be good students, good friends, good teammates, good employees, and, most importantly, good parents to their own kids so the cycle will not repeat itself.

Action Plan #1

Gender balance in elementary schools. Today in almost every elementary school in the US, we are way out of gender balance. We provide little, if any, male role models in the formative and developmental years for boys. Kids can almost go through their entire elementary school experience without a single male teacher. If they do get a male teacher, it's generally in the 4th or 5th grade and it may be only one. This is a tremendous disservice to boys that needs to be abruptly and quickly changed. Elementary schools should have a 50-50 balance of male teachers to female teachers just as high schools and generally most middle schools do. Having constant lack of male role models provides poor messages to boys, sends improper signals and promotes behaviors that boys have difficulty identifying with. This is a tragedy that needs to be corrected.

Action Plan #2

Bring back recess. Normal boys need to exercise in elementary school at least three times per day. Most of our nation's older population experienced a morning, lunch, and afternoon recess. Because of NCLB and other accountability issues, recess has been eliminated in the morning and afternoon. Most elementary kids around the US average about 1.1 periods of recess per week. It would be hard for most adults to sit still and listen to a teacher in a classroom from 9am to noon, without much of a break. And then repeat that cycle in the afternoon. That's a lot to ask a 2nd and 3rd grader to do without the ability to move around and blow off steam. Boys need this, it is important for their brain development, social emotional growth, and their ability to concentrate and learn. It is a travesty that with an obese society (one out of every three children is clinically obese), that we can't get our students outside to enjoy leisure activities, move around, exercise, and soak up some Vitamin D from the sun. This needs to be changed if we want to keep at-risk boys in school.

Action Plan #3

Mandate gender training for new teachers. Walk into any of the great educational colleges around the US and looking at their course selection list. You will find NOTHING offered in gender training for teachers. There will be no classes in differences between how boys and girls learn, there will be no classes in differences between how conflict resolution is handled between boys and girls, and no classes on differences in the way girls and boys learn to write and grasp a pen. Rather, teachers are left to fend for themselves and learn as they go.

Action Plan #4

Mandate kinesthetic learning techniques for core subjects. If we are really interested in helping boys learn better, along with girls, then we need the use of kinesthetic, hands on approach for our five core subjects. This would include math, science, social studies, reading, and writing. Having students use their hands and be involved with active participation and a kinesthetic hands-on approach will greatly increase their interest, memory, retention, and ability to comprehend important subjects. Having young boys learn simple arithmetic through hop-scotch or other motor activities greatly improves their ability to comprehend subjects and promotes greater long-term retention. There is an over reliance of auditory delivery system in elementary schools for all students. This greatly reduces boys' ability to comprehend without putting a greater reliance on body motion to learn important functional core subjects.

Action Plan #5

One required season on a sports team in middle school and high school. Each student would greatly benefit from a season on a sports team in middle school and high school. This ability to be on a sports team without having to worry about getting cut or being eliminated would help students learn very important life lessons. The ability to know how to win and how to lose, how to show emotion, how to show praise, how to deal with both negative and positive concepts and setbacks, and learning to work with teammates on a common theme is hugely important, especially for boys. It also helps boys learn appropriate ways to handle their warlock gene issues. Asking students to participate in a 14-week sports season, one time in middle school and one time in high school, would provide huge social emotional gains for boys. Team sports teach young people how to cope in the real world, in employment settings where many people work together in functioning collaborative teams.

Action Plan #6

Eliminate elementary school pods seating. The most confusing message that we send to the boys in elementary school is pod seating. We put 6 desks together and place 6 individuals in this grouping of desks where they face each other. Not only does it make it difficult to concentrate, but students look at each other's work and seldom are asked to do things in groups. Teachers sometimes promote team work in these pods, yet grading of test and other assignments is based on individual performance. It would be much better for boys to learn appropriate concentration skills by having individual seating. There is nothing wrong with desks in rows and having a dedicated individual work space at an individual desk. This is what American society is about in our K-12 systems and students are asked to excel at their individual performance of instructional goals. It is much easier for boys to reflect in individual seating. Pod seating sends confusing and confounding messages to all students.

Action Plan #7

Make a grade for social emotional intelligence. We spend 12 years grading students on their knowledge of social studies, the war of 1812, and the American Revolution. Yet when they go out to the work place, seldom will they need this information. It falls back to the facts, figures, and fudge. Yet students will need their abilities to mature, work individually, and motivate themselves to work with other students. This needs to be graded and reinforced in school. Grades should be given for the ability to self-motivate, pay attention, and problem solve. These are extremely important assets yet we never give them individual grades for performance. This is about one's own ability to be socially mature. Some of our average students who graduate from elementary, middle, high school and college end up being whirlwinds in the business world. That is because their social emotional IQ is so high. This needs to be rewarded and promoted in our K-12 schools and not left to parents, because most parents won't.

<u>Action Plan #8</u>

Gender-specific classes in elementary school for boys and girls in reading and writing. The most difficult subjects for boys are reading and writing. Most boys' fine motor dexterity has not developed to a point where they can even put ideas on paper. We also have test scores and assessment pieces being introduced too quickly in elementary schools, for both girls and boys. It would be better to put girls and boys in gender specific reading and writing classes in 1st-4th grade. This would allow teachers to focus on generic things that could help boys pick up and move forward to match their female counterparts.

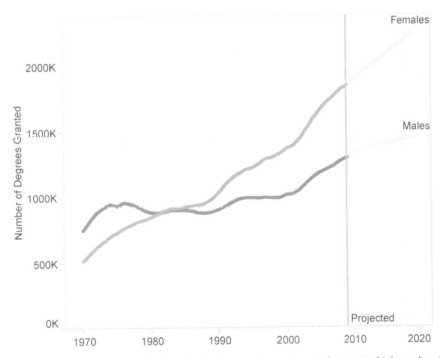

College Degrees by Gender
1970 to 2019 (2009 to 2019 projected)

(**Source:** http://www.aei-ideas.org/2010/05/the-huge-and-growing-gender-gap-in-higher-education/)

Action Plan #9

B-WIP (Boys Warlock Individualized Plan) Under the BWIP, each student, as they go through the middle school and high school, would develop their own individualized reflective plan on how to deal with their power oriented gene, the gene to conquer. Will they find ways to appropriately channel this energy through leisure and rec, through writing, through sports, or through chess matches? Whatever the plan is, it needs to be written out and dealt with to cut down on aggressive acts, road rage, and other aggressive activities which boys so often display. It will cut down on physical altercations and the like if boys are given the time to develop a plan and reflect upon it to find appropriate ways to channel their energy. This is long overdue and needs to again be reinforced by K-12 schools. Each kid would graduate with a BWIP plan that should be hung on the wall someplace where they can look at it on a daily basis.

Action Plan #10

Mandate that all students attend a conflict resolution class in middle school and high school. In order to graduate, students must pass a reflective conflict resolution plan that focuses on the social emotional piece. Conflict resolution and social emotional growth, not instruction, should be number 1 in our schools. Facts, figures and fudge in our information society can be found at the touch of a laptop, cell phone, or picture phone. Technology has made information accessible to all. Students have ways to access this information readily through technology, calculators, and all sorts of miniature computers. What must be reinforced and replaced as our number one priority are social emotional development and conflict resolution classes. These should be given the same weight and status as a student's English, reading, and math classes.

Conclusion

American culture is embedded with a competitive spirit that finds its way into K-12 public education. We have identified this clearly throughout the book as a sorting and selecting process in K-12 public schools. For the vast majority of students this process is healthy and replicates the greater competitive spirit of our democratic society. However, this competitive spirit needs a line in the sand to assist the at-risk and special education boys. A no contest approach is the ultimate answer for the at-risk group of boys that exist within our public schools. This group of boys, approximately 15-25% of the male student body, needs full cooperation, support, emotional parachutes, and rescue techniques that avoid all issues of competition. This group has already identified itself as the lower performing section of our schools. Rather than let them fail, drop out and cause staggering implications to resources, these boys need to be rescued and set on proper employment and leisure and recreation pathways. Throughout multiple decades we have placed great stock in to schools to solve societal ills such as substance abuse, bullying, nutrition, etc. We have clearly failed to address this as a singular gender issue. A new approach needs to be clearly directed for this at-risk, male population who often commit acts of violence, criminal activities and are generally detrimental to society. This answer lies in the connectedness between adults and our ethical duty to help these needy boys. A new frontier needs to occur that elevates their social-emotional status through the connectedness of activities, sports and adult mentorship; rather than the current trend of emotional disposal.

Derrick R. Fries Biography

Derrick Fries is an Associate Professor at Eastern Michigan University in the Department of Special Education. Following his doctoral degree in Educational Administration at the University of Michigan in 1993, Dr. Fries became the principal of Avondale Middle School in Auburn Hills, Michigan. In 2001, Avondale Middle School became a Blue Ribbon Exemplary School under Dr. Fries' leadership. In 2002, Dr. Fries became Deputy Superintendent of Avondale Schools where he held the positions of Special Education Director, Community Education Director and K-12 Curriculum Director. In 2006 after beginning his tenure-track professorship at EMU, Fries began an extensive research project examining the consequences of the new Michigan Merit Curriculum and its ultimate effects on high school graduation rates.

Dr. Fries is one of few educators in Michigan to have earned both Oakland County Teacher of the Year (1986) and Michigan Middle School Regional Principal of the Year (2001) during his 31 year K-12 public school career. Dr. Fries was also a NASA Teacher in Space finalist in 1986 and is the author of the world's most famous Learn to Sail book entitled *Start Sailing Right.* This book is now owned by US SAILING and is translated into six different languages. In 2006, Fries was nominated into the International Sailing World Hall of Fame. From 1975 to 2001 he won 6 Sailing World Titles and 15 National/North American Titles. He was a Collegiate All-American in Sailing in 1973 and 1974 while attending Michigan State University. He is also a triathlete and a past professional sailor. During the summers of 2008, 09, 10, 11, 12 & 13 he has competed in over 87 triathlons and is a United States Triathlon Association "All-American." Since 1979 he has been mentoring boys and their connectedness to sports activities. This includes both at-risk students and special education students. He is currently the Autism Spectrum Graduate Coordinator for Eastern Michigan University.

Sources:

William Pollock, Real Boys (New York: Henry Holt and Company, 1998).

Dr. James Dobson, Bringing up Boys (USA: James Dobson, Inc., 2001).

Steve Biddulph, Raising Boys (Canada: Ten Speed Canada, 1998).

Robert Sylwester, A Biological Brain in a Cultural Classroom (Thousand Oaks, California: Corwin Press, Inc., 2000).

Richard Whitmire, Why Boys Fail: Saving our Sons from an Educational System that's Leaving Them Behind (New York, New York: Richard Whitmire, 2010).

Works Cited:

No Child Left Behind (NCLB) Act of 2001, 20 U.S.C.A. § 6301 et seq. (West 2003).

National Center for Education Statistics, 2013, Public High School Graduation Rates, Retrieved from < http://nces.ed.gov/programs/coe/indicator_coi.asp>.

Michigan Center for Educational Performance & Information, 2012, State of Michigan 2012 Cohort Four-Year, 2011 Cohort Five-Year and 2010 Six-Year Graduation and Dropout Rate including Subgroups, Retrieved from <http://www.michigan.gov/cepi/0,1607,7-113-21423_30451_51357---,00.html>.

Grall, Timothy; United States Census Bureau, 2011, Custodial Mothers and Fathers and Their Child Support: 2009, Retrieved from <http://www.census.gov/prod/2011pubs/p60-240.pdf>.

Bloom B, Cohen RA, Freeman G; Summary Health Statistics for U.S. Children: National Health Interview Survey, 2011. National Center for Health Statistics. Vital Health Stat 10(254). 2012. Retrieved from <http://www.cdc.gov/nchs/data/series/sr_10/sr10_254.pdf>.